DESPERATE PRAYERS *for* DESPERATE TIMES

JOHN ECKHARDT

Most Charisma House Book Group products are available at special quantity discounts for bulk purchase for sales promotions, premiums, fund-raising, and educational needs. For details, write Charisma House Book Group, 600 Rinehart Road, Lake Mary, Florida 32746, or telephone (407) 333-0600.

Desperate Prayers for Desperate Times
by John Eckhardt
Published by Charisma House
Charisma Media/Charisma House Book Group
600 Rinehart Road
Lake Mary, Florida 32746
www.charismahouse.com

Visit the author's website at www.johneckhardt.global.

Library of Congress Cataloging-in-Publication Data:
Names: Eckhardt, John, 1957- author.
Title: Desperate prayers for desperate times / John Eckhardt.
Description: Lake Mary, Florida : Charisma House, 2018. | Includes bibliographical references.
Identifiers: LCCN 2018021678 (print) | LCCN 2018025026 (ebook) | ISBN 9781629995366 (ebook) | ISBN 9781629995359 (trade paper)
Subjects: LCSH: Prayer--Christianity.
Classification: LCC BV210.3 (ebook) | LCC BV210.3 .E278 2018 (print) | DDC 248.3/2--dc23
LC record available at https://lccn.loc.gov/2018021678

While the author has made every effort to provide accurate internet addresses at the time of publication, neither the publisher nor the author assumes any responsibility for errors or for changes that occur after publication. Further, the publisher does not have any control over and does not assume any responsibility for author or third-party websites or their content.

18 19 20 21 22 — 987654321
Printed in the United States of America

Contents

Introduction

The Prayers of the Desperate Avail Much

> The eyes of the LORD are on the righteous.... [They] cry out, and the LORD hears, and delivers them out of all their troubles. The LORD is near to the broken-hearted, and saves the contrite of spirit. Many are the afflictions of the righteous, but the LORD delivers him out of them all.
>
> —PSALM 34:15–19

WE ALL GO through hard times—some more desperate than others. Sometimes we look over into other people's lives and it seems like things are going well, but even they have trouble. None of us is exempt. As the Bible says, He "sends rain on the just and on the unjust" (Matt. 5:45), and what we suffer is common among all people (1 Cor. 10:13). But as a believer you have a special advantage. Because of Jesus, you can boldly approach the throne of God and find help in your time of need. You do not have to wait for permission. You don't have to wait for someone else to pray for you. You can go before God and petition for His grace, favor, comfort, strategy, help, wisdom, encouragement, and answers for yourself. And what I've come to tell you is that when you pray, He hears you. He will come and answer and deliver you from all of your troubles.

But this is something you already know. You picked up this book because you are facing a season in your life like none other. You may not have ever seen times like this. What you are facing is something that has been showing up on your prayer list day after day, month after month, and year after year. You know that God hears you, but somehow the answer, the breakthrough, the release has not come, and you are getting more desperate by the day to hear from God.

It has been some years since I last wrote a book on prayer, but being a pastor and traveling the world, I've become acquainted with the prayers of the saints. The prayers and cries of the people of God from around the world for God to intervene on their behalf have motivated me to write this book, which I pray will be a tool and resource we can use to bring us victory in our most challenging and difficult times.

There seems to be trouble on every side for some of us—long-term illness, financial struggles, addiction, abuse, relationship problems, and loved ones who are far from God. We are also praying for fruitfulness, expansion, and increase in our callings and ministries—and not just for our benefit. We have a burden to bring forth the glory and majesty of God in our lives in order to impact the world around us. We know that when God brings deliverance and blessing to our lives, we are then able to be a blessing to others. So we pray, day after day, month after month, and year after year, asking, seeking, and knocking.

What's the Holdup?

If we realize that God knows our needs before we even pray about them and that if He hears our prayers we have what we have asked, what could be the holdup in this particular area you've been praying about for so long? Where is the breakthrough? Where is the manifestation? Where is the increase? Where is the fruit? Where is the healing?

In this book we are going to look at several scenarios that may apply to where you are with God in this time of desperation. Most of the delay in prayer has to do with demonic forces, of course. Then there are other circumstances when we have made bad decisions and have to deal with the consequences. And still in other cases, God is delaying our breakthrough in order to bring us to a place where we can handle the thing He is trying to bring about in our lives.

To bring revelation to what God may be doing in your life, we are going to look at the life of Hannah. In her time of desperation, anguish, and torment in praying for a son, God was leading her to make a vow. We are going to look at the people of Israel and what God needed to do in their lives before they crossed the Jordan and went into the Promised Land. Then we are going to explore the reign of King Josiah and what God needed to purge from the land before the temple could be restored to its full function and purpose. We are also going to see what happens in heaven when the prayers of the saints reach a tipping point and how those prayers are instrumental in bringing relief from the desperate times all over the world.

The Blessing of Desperation

Believe it or not, there are blessings that come in seasons of desperation. Without these seasons we would not be able to build the spiritual strength and character we need to withstand the weight of God's glory. Neither would we have the depth of anointing needed to minister to others and bring the glory of God to the nations.

God desires to bring restoration and revival to every aspect of our lives. It is also His ultimate plan to fill the earth with His glory. And I love that it is our desperate prayers that bring it all to pass.

If you are desperate for God to answer a long-overdue prayer, if you feel that He has forgotten you, and if it seems your destiny, dreams, purpose, and vision are held up or will not manifest, I want to encourage you not to give in to the voice of the enemy. God does hear your prayers. He will answer. He will help you. He will deliver you and bring His plans to pass in your life. Keep asking. Keep seeking. Keep knocking. It is often at your lowest point that you are closest to your greatest miracle.

Prayer Strategies for Desperate Times

This book will show you five major prayer strategies that show up in the lives of men and women of God whose backs were against the wall. They prayed prayers that got results, and through their times of desperation they learned to do the following:

1. Get even more desperate. Don't hide your feelings from God. Get to the house of God, the

house of worship, and pour your heart out to Him. I am reminded of the time King David said, "I will become even more undignified than this, and I will be humiliated in my own eyes" (2 Sam. 6:22, NIV), in response to his wife's judgment of his actions in the presence of the Lord. Don't let people tell you it doesn't take all that praying and worshipping and crying and dancing to get God's attention. Sometimes you need to get loud for God to hear you over the crowd and for Him to walk in your direction and ask, "What do you want Me to do for you?" (See Luke 18:35–43.)

2. Persevere. Don't give up or give in to the taunts and torment of the enemy. Keep pressing and praying. Your prayers will reach a tipping point in heaven, and angels will be released to act in the heavenlies on your behalf.

3. Seek God's presence. As you seek God, He will reveal to you the truth of His Word. He will give you direction about the things that need to be purged from your life so you can be restored and revived.

4. Make a vow to God and keep it. All that God does for His people is based on covenant. The faithful ones receive the blessing of His covenant instead of the curses. Recommitting

yourself to God is a way to have the blessings of heaven poured out over your life.

5. Prophesy. As you come out of the wilderness, and as God brings deliverance in answer to your prayers, you will be filled with joy and gladness. Your faith will grow to new levels, and you will begin to believe God beyond what He has done for you. You will begin to see visions of God's favor, mercy, and, most of all, His glory reaching out to the ends of the earth. You will begin to believe that the desperate times we are facing as a planet will be eradicated.

I have also included prayers and declarations at the end of each chapter to help you pray through what the Lord reveals to you about the strategies presented. The one thing you want to develop more than anything else in your life as a believer is your prayer life. Prayer is the primary way that we talk to and hear God. It is the gateway to worship, prophecy, direction, wisdom, and so much more. This book will help you to become strong in prayer no matter what situations you face in life.

Desperate Prayers Give You the Last Word Over the Enemy

When all options are exhausted and everything you were holding on to has failed, God steps in. He hears your cries.

He has not forgotten His promise to you. He never turns away the desperate. Your days of weeping are over.

No matter where you are in your life, how bad things may look, or what situation you find yourself in, I am here to let you know that you will prophesy again. You will have the last word over the enemy.

God is the same yesterday, today, and forever. He didn't give us the stories in the Bible to put us to sleep at night. He gave them to us to build our faith in the impossible and so that we can declare, "If He did it for Hannah, Josiah, David, the people of Israel, and the blind beggar on the roadside, He will do it for me!"

God likes shutting up the devil. God doesn't like when evil and wickedness torment the lives of His people. He is righteous and holy and will break the power of the enemy. When God sees you in your desperate condition, He looks upon you with mercy and compassion. He heals the brokenhearted. He lifts up the lowly. He looks out for those who are down and have no bread. To those who are weak, He says, "I will give you My strength."

This book is for desperate people in desperate situations who can't go on if God doesn't step in and do something miraculous—quickly. I pray that what you read in these next several chapters will give you what you need to press in more, persist more, and believe more for the miracles God will perform in response to this season you are facing. Let God do His work in you so that you can experience a level of blessing that outmatches the troubles you will overcome.

Chapter 1

Your Name Is Favor

> So Hannah arose after they had eaten in Shiloh and after they had drunk. Now Eli the priest was sitting on a seat by the door of the tabernacle of the LORD. And she was bitter, and prayed to the LORD, and wept severely. So she made a vow and said, "O LORD of Hosts, if You will indeed look on the affliction of Your maidservant, and remember me and not forget Your maidservant, but will give to Your maidservant a baby boy, then I will give him to the LORD all the days of his life, and no razor shall touch his head."
>
> —1 SAMUEL 1:9–11

HANNAH IS ONE of the most recognizable women in the Bible. She is remembered as an amazing woman and the mother of one of Israel's greatest prophets. But before she was recognized in history as such, her situation looked bleak. In the Hebrew culture at that time, as well as in many cultures today, it was believed that a woman was blessed if she had a large number of children. If she was infertile or barren, it was a sign that she was not blessed. Hannah's husband, Elkanah, had two wives. His other wife, Peninnah, had children while Hannah did not. In her community Hannah was considered a failure, forgotten, or cursed by God.

To make matters worse, Peninnah tormented and mocked Hannah because Hannah had no children. Her adversary was the other wife. Can you imagine? It is not an ideal situation for any woman to have to share her husband with another woman. I would imagine that most women would have a hard time if their husband came home with a second wife. The response wouldn't only be, "Oh, no! She's not moving in!" It would most likely also be, "You're moving out!" However, in Hannah's time, it was common for wealthy men to have more than one wife. David had many wives, eight of whom were named in the Bible.[1] His son Solomon had seven hundred wives and three hundred concubines—one thousand women (1 Kings 11:3)! No wonder he left out of here crazy![2]

As we can see from many stories in the Bible, when there is more than one woman involved in a marriage situation and one cannot bear children, there is a lot of jealousy, taunting, and strife. Consider the stories of Rachel and Leah (Gen. 29:31–30:24) and Sarah and Hagar (Gen. 16:1–9; 21:9–12). The shame of being barren in these cases and even into our modern times can be overwhelming. This is where we enter Hannah's story.

When Your Life Doesn't Look Like Your Name

What's interesting about Hannah is that despite what was happening to her in the natural, her name carries special meaning in the spirit. In Hebrew her name means "grace," and it is derived from another Hebrew word, *chanan*, which means "favor" or "favored."[3] The name Hannah is a variation of the name Anna, who was a praying prophet in the New Testament. Anna also prayed and fasted in the temple night and day and prophesied about the birth of a child—Jesus, who was also called the great Prophet (Luke 7:16), like Samuel was. Both names—Hannah and Anna—mean grace and favor.

Just to remind you, in both Hebrew and Greek the words translated as "grace" are connected to God's acceptance, loving-kindness, goodwill, and mercy given to us.[4] They are also used in connection with the special abilities believers receive from the Holy Spirit that enable us to help draw people into the kingdom. We call them gifts of the Spirit. (See 1 Corinthians 12.) The Greek word for *gifts* in this context is *charisma*, which means "divine grace."[5]

Grace is closely connected to favor.

Favor is defined as "approval, support, or liking for someone or something; an act of kindness beyond what is due or usual; [to] feel or show approval or preference for; (often used in polite requests) give someone (something desired)."[6] It means "to give special regard to; to treat with goodwill; to show exceptional kindness to someone. Sometimes, it means to show extra kindness in comparison to the treatment of others; that is, preferential treatment."[7] Favor is also "friendly regard shown toward another especially by a superior; gracious kindness; an act of such kindness; aid, assistance."[8] To a Christian, favor with God is what He bestows upon you or gives you.

When someone uses their power, influence, position,

wealth, authority, and words to help and bless you, that is favor—and it doesn't depend on anything you've done. Favor is unmerited, meaning you don't deserve it, but it is given to you anyway. God is a God of favor; He loves to bless His people simply because He is a good Father.[9]

Knowing what we know about Hannah, and after understanding what *grace* and *favor* mean, it is strange to encounter Hannah in 1 Samuel 1 at the beginning of her story, when she is experiencing neither grace nor favor. Realize that people during this time named their children based on what happened at the time of their birth or with special insight into their character. Therefore, we can come to the conclusion that grace and favor were the essence of Hannah's identity. Her father or mother saw that grace was a part of who she was or would be. She was favored by God. His grace was to be upon her life.

But at the beginning of 1 Samuel 1, it does not seem as though Hannah is experiencing grace or favor from God, because her womb was shut up. She had no children. I imagine Hannah saying, "My name is favor, but it seems as if God has not favored me. Here's another woman who has children, and she torments me." From her perspective, this was not the favor of God that she was supposed to live out.

So what do you do when it seems as though your life is not being lived in the way that reflects the name you were given or, maybe more relatable to us in this time, the call of God on your life? You are chosen, called out, anointed, and in covenant with God. You are the favored of the Lord. His favor, grace, and blessing should be apparent in your life. But here you are—no productivity, no fruitfulness, no increase, and no multiplication. Your name is

Hannah. Your name is favor. Your name is grace. But there is no demonstration of the favor or grace of God in your life. It looks like everything in your life is the opposite of what it should be. And to make things worse, the enemy is mocking and tormenting you. This was Hannah's condition. The devil was using Peninnah to mock, laugh at, and torment Hannah.

Peninnah is an example of how the devil can speak through people and cause them to be so cruel. Under his influence, people have no compassion and can be so arrogant and unmerciful. Peninnah was saying, "Look at me. I have plenty of children. Look at you; you have nothing. You're barren." Sometimes when you're in a bad situation, people say things to you and don't realize they are being used by the enemy.

Be careful not to be a Peninnah.

Sometimes we are the Peninnahs in other people's lives. We hope and pray with Hannah-like desires but don't realize that bitterness has set in due to our deferred hope. Or we may have already received our miracle but forgotten what the waiting time was like.

Whatever your position, be careful not to mock, and don't despise people who are going through trials. You may end up looking up to them when God takes them from the low place to the high place. Be careful who you laugh at. Sometimes pride causes those of us who are doing well to laugh at those who are not doing well. Sometimes those of us who are blessed will point the finger at others who don't seem to be blessed, saying they're nobodies. But God is the One who weighs the actions and the hearts of people.

Do you know what else I've learned from this story after reading and studying it many times? Despite the mocking, tormenting, and laughing—anything the enemy means for evil—God can turn it all around for your good. I love that about Him. He takes nobodies, those whom the devil laughs at, those whom the devil beats down, those who feel like they are losers and like there is no hope, and those who feel like they will never be anything and that giving up is the best option—He takes those particular people, changes their situation, and gives them a miracle.

It's Time to Reclaim Your Name

There is a point in the process when you can get worn down from standing in faith against the attacks of the enemy. The Bible says that Hannah was "in bitterness of soul" (1 Sam. 1:10, KJV) from constantly hearing accusations of failure. This means that she was in deep depression. She was brokenhearted. She had a heart full of grief. She was sad and deeply distressed, and she couldn't shake those feelings.

Have you ever had people tell you to just shake it, and you try to shake it, but you can't? Maybe they say, "Be strong. Don't worry. It's going to be all right. Believe God." And maybe you do believe God, but you are still in bitterness of soul over your current state. Of course it doesn't help that the enemy stays in your face telling you you're a failure, you're barren. And let's not forget that you are aware of whom you have been called to be in the midst of the hardship. Your name is favor, but in this season your life isn't lining up with that name.

I want to encourage you here with something I believe

Hannah held on to despite her feelings: God had not forgotten her, and God has not forgotten you. It may seem as though God is blessing everybody except you, even the unrighteous. You are serving, tithing, worshipping, praying, prophesying, speaking in tongues, running up and down the aisle, and waving flags. You have swords of the Spirit out, poking demons. You're lifting your hands. You're turning around telling five folks, "I've got the victory." You're living clean. You resist temptation. You haven't walked away from God. You are doing everything you know to do, but it looks like there's still no breakthrough in your life. But God has a plan. For a season God lets the enemy think you're going lose, but like He did with His Son, He will cause your dreams and desires to be resurrected with a whole new level of power.

Remember, in the spirit your very name is favor, and it is time to reclaim your name. Even though it looks as though there's no favor in your life and things are not changing, if you call upon the Lord, He will answer you. If you ask, you will receive. If you seek, you will find. If you knock, it will be opened to you.

I believe when the Bible says, "So Hannah rose up…" (1 Sam. 1:9, KJV), was when Hannah regained the boldness and courage to go after what she knew was hers. In 1 Samuel 1:7–11 we can see five specific actions Hannah took to reclaim the promise of her name and release a new level of fruitfulness in her life. These are the actions you will need to take as well.

1. Don't give up.

> This man [Elkanah] went up out of his city annually to worship and to sacrifice to the LORD of Hosts in Shiloh.... Now her [Hannah's] rival [Peninnah] provoked her greatly, making her miserable because the LORD had closed her womb. Thus it was yearly, when she went up to the house of the LORD, that she provoked her. So Hannah wept and did not eat.
>
> —1 SAMUEL 1:3, 6–7

The Bible says that yearly Hannah, Elkanah, and Peninnah would go to the temple to offer sacrifices. Yearly Hannah was without child. Yearly Peninnah tormented her, and yearly Hannah put her petition for a son before the Lord. Hannah did not give up. Previously we discussed what it's like to feel weighed down by the onslaught of attacks from the enemy combined with the feeling of not having your prayers answered. I mentioned briefly that God has a plan in this for us. A lot of times, we lose perspective in the midst of the battle. Sometimes the battle wages long, and we want to give up. This is what the enemy wants you to do. He is hoping you will get tired and quit. He wants us to doubt God. He wants us to get discouraged about our power and authority over him. He wants us to lose sight of the reality that through Christ, we already have the victory.

I believe that God is going to give you a new level of strength and courage to endure. You may be wondering why God would allow you to live through such a difficult season. It has been my experience that God allows us to go through certain seasons for a period of time to teach us how to fight. The Bible says that God trains our hands for war (Ps. 144:1). In seasons like the one Hannah was in, we learn valuable lessons in persistence and faith. God wants us to learn how to stand in Him and the power of His might (Eph. 6:10). As the saying goes, with each new level He brings you to, there is a new level of demonic opposition. Some of the men and women of God we admire—giants in the faith—had to overcome significant hardships to arrive at the place we see them in.

This is the core lesson in Hannah's story: She did not give up. Year after year, in the face of endless taunts, mocking, and accusation, she continued her pursuit for what she knew the Lord willed for her life.

2. Fast.

First Samuel 1:7–8 says that "yearly, when she went up to the house of the LORD…she [Peninnah] provoked her. So Hannah wept and did not eat. Then said Elkanah her husband to her, 'Hannah, why are you weeping? And why do you not eat?'"

In my book *God's Covenant With You for Deliverance and Freedom*, I talk about times when we are in a long war against stubborn demons.[10] Barrenness, infertility, unfruitfulness, and unproductivity—both in the natural and in the spirit—are stubborn demons that can plague a person year after year, as they did Hannah. As God's Word suggests, we should take the attacks of these demonic spirits seriously, just as Hannah did. She saw that these demons came to steal the seed of the word of the Lord over her life, so she went into a season of fasting. She did not eat. Perhaps she saw that what she was up against would not "come out except by prayer and fasting" (Mark 9:29).

I realize that this part of her situation could be read in a way that suggests she wasn't eating because she was so burdened by her condition. But I believe the Lord put this here so that we could take from Hannah's story both interpretations and realize that if we want to see a demon as stubborn as barrenness broken off our lives, we need to push back from the table, sacrifice a meal or two or however many it takes, get alone with God, and pray.

Fasting has a way of humbling our flesh and allowing the Spirit of God to arise within us. As we are humbled before Him and awaiting our victory, His grace can be our strength. The Bible says that "God resists the proud, but gives grace to the humble" (James 4:6).

Hannah was at her lowest, and she reduced herself even more when she fasted. She was positioning herself to be restored to living according to the full meaning of her name. She was getting in position to have the grace and favor of God released into her life.

3. Worship and weep.

> Once after a sacrificial meal at Shiloh, Hannah got up and went to pray. Eli the priest was sitting at his customary place beside the entrance of the Tabernacle. Hannah was in deep anguish, crying bitterly as she prayed to the LORD.
>
> —1 SAMUEL 1:9–10, NLT

The word *tabernacle* in this verse also means "temple" or "sanctuary," which is why you see it translated differently depending on the Bible version you read.[11] The sanctuary of God, the temple, or the house of the Lord is where

His presence dwells. If you know anything about being in the presence of God, then you know you can come broken, anguished, and in deep "bitterness of soul" (v. 10, KJV) and know that you will be met with His miraculous glory.

Worship is the gateway to the glory of God, and there are many forms of worship. Some include the shedding of tears and deep supplication as we come recognizing the greatness of who He is and that He is all-powerful and all-knowing. I see this demonstrated in *barak* worship, which is expressed through kneeling and bowing before the Lord, crying out for His deliverance.[12] (See Psalm 72:12–15.)

Worship is often equated with joy, but sometimes in our darkest times we must choose to enter the presence of God despite how we feel. In an article titled "Weeping in Worship," Emily Barnhardt says this:

> Worship has the power to gently touch a bleeding place of deep, aching despair within us, in a way that activates a persevering hope in our minds and in our spirits, amidst that pain. Worship, alone, enables us to lift our eyes above deep sorrow, to gaze at Him, instead. And gazing at Him reminds us of His character, His goodness, and His promises, which leads us to joy—a type of joy that can surpass all understanding and overpower even the deepest depths of our grief and pain.[13]

In seasons like this, our recognition of His place over our troubles and approaching Him with this awareness is worship. Hannah worshipped, wept, and cried out to the Lord in His holy temple. She came to the house of the Lord and made her request known to Him because she knew He was the only One who had the power to deliver her.

We can count on God's glory to be the place where there is healing of all our diseases, restoration from the desolation of the enemy, and even fruitfulness for the barren. Hannah had a relationship with God and knew that if she wanted to see her hopes and dreams realized, she needed to get in His presence.

This is why I am excited to go into the house of God every week. The release of God's glory in His sanctuary is one of the more miraculous and life-giving things we can experience as believers. The opportunity we have to experience the glory and presence of God in His temple is validation enough for the verse that encourages us not to "forsake the assembling of ourselves together" (Heb. 10:25). I know there are some who feel like they don't have to come to a physical building to worship, and that's fine. We know that because of the coming of the Holy Spirit (Acts 2), we are now ourselves temples (1 Cor. 6:19). But let's not overlook the power of God that is released in corporate worship in an alive and glory-filled church.

If you have been wrestling in prayer and desire to see tremendous breakthrough in your life, get to a church that does not hinder the flow of God's presence and glory and begin to cry out to God, recognizing His power, majesty, and glory.

4. Pray.

> And she...prayed to the LORD.
>
> —1 SAMUEL 1:10

As part of her worship and in the midst of her weeping, Hannah prayed. Philippians 4:6–7 says, "Be anxious for nothing, but in everything, by prayer and supplication with gratitude, make your requests known to God. And the peace of God, which surpasses all understanding, will protect your hearts and minds through Christ Jesus." Hannah was not only going after what she desired; she was also pursuing peace. Year after year she had been discouraged and beaten down. Anxiety may have tried to get her to focus on Peninnah and her lack, but Hannah remained steadfast in putting her requests before the Lord.

The Bible says that when Hannah prayed, her lips moved but no sound came out, and the priest thought she was drunk (1 Sam. 1:13). She let him know that she was not drunk, but after having poured out her soul to the Lord in such heavy grief for as long as she had, I imagine that there was not much more she had words for. Now she only prayed from deep within, from a silent place of desperation.

We know that God hears what people can't hear. Not everyone will hear your deepest cry when you are in such anguish that you don't even know what to say. God doesn't need words. God looks at the heart. And when God sees your condition, He comes and answers you.

5. Make a vow of surrender.

When it looks like everything is falling apart and you have no strength, joy, or power, that's when God says, "Now I can step in with My strength and power. Now I can do for you what you cannot do for yourself." Our God is a God of miracles. Our God is the God of breakthrough. Our God is a God who will not despise your condition if you cry out to Him in surrender.

I will talk about why this is one of the most significant aspects of Hannah's story in the next chapter, as it is tied to being in a place of desperation, but I want to touch on it here because this was the last step Hannah took just before the man of God pronounced a blessing over her that God would grant her request (1 Sam. 1:17). She made a vow to God that if He would give her a son, she would give him back to God.

> So she made a vow and said, "O LORD of Hosts, if You will indeed look on the affliction of Your maidservant, and remember me and not forget Your maidservant, but will give to Your maidservant a baby boy, then I will give him to the LORD all the days of his life, and no razor shall touch his head."
>
> —1 SAMUEL 1:11

Sometimes one of the most powerful things you can do is to make a vow to God and keep it: "God, if You do this for me, I'll serve You. I'll worship You all the days of my life." Don't ever make a vow and forget to keep your promise when God grants your request. Hannah's desperation was matched by her gratefulness to God when He granted her petition. She kept her vow and birthed one of the greatest prophets Israel had ever known. She received the answer to her prayers, and Israel experienced one of the greatest prophetic movements in its history. For seventy years before Samuel came on the scene, Israel had not heard from God. Through prayer Hannah not only received what she wanted; she also opened a portal to the heavenlies.

In doing these five things Hannah drew the favor of God back into her life like a magnet. Pursuing God and what He has for you without quitting; fasting, which brings humility; worshipping; praying; and making a commitment of surrender and obedience open the heavens so the favor of God will return to your life. I call them favor magnets. Other ways you can begin to attract favor into your life include living with integrity, giving, extending mercy, exercising wisdom, dwelling in the glory of God, engaging in praise and worship, and living with humility, faith, and righteousness. Meditate on these actions. Investigate how Hannah exhibited them. Then ask God for wisdom and courage to carry out these actions in your life.

You Will Prophesy Again

First Samuel 2 is Hannah's prophetic declaration to the nations of God's faithfulness. God had opened her womb, and she bore a son, just as she desired. So now in 1 Samuel 2:1 she begins to testify and proclaim the goodness of the Lord and His faithfulness to deliver His people out of all their troubles. She says, "My heart rejoices in the LORD; my horn is exalted in the LORD. My mouth is bold against my enemies, because I rejoice in Your salvation." The King James Version put it this way: "My mouth is enlarged over mine enemies; because I rejoice in thy salvation." In other words, you will have the last word. The enemy has been talking and talking, but God is about to bring you to a place of victory and authority, to where your mouth is going to be enlarged over your enemies.

Listen, God does not put these stories in the Bible for

our entertainment. God wants to show us the record of His faithfulness from one generation to the next. He wants us to know that what He did for them in the past He will do for us now. His Word and the testimonies of the saints are proof of that. He is saying, "I'm the same God then as I am now. I still do miracles now, and I put Hannah's story in My Word so you can read it and be encouraged."

God doesn't like ugly.

Look at 1 Samuel 2:2. It starts with, "There is none holy as the LORD." This verse points out one of my favorite things about God: He is righteous. His righteousness won't allow people to be mistreated without consequences. It's not in the Bible, but my mother used to say, "God don't like ugly." It's true. God does not like when we mistreat each other. When you think about what you've been through and the people in your life who were like Peninnah in Hannah's, know that God is watching and He doesn't like what's been happening. So in essence He says, "I don't just deliver you for you. I also do it because I don't like what the enemy has done to you. He's been a bully. He's been beating up on you."

When God sees people who have been beaten up, beaten down, and tormented, He takes it personally. He says, "I'll be your Defender. I'll be your Savior. I'll be your Deliverer. I'll step in when you can't fight your own battle. I'll say, 'The battle is not yours; it belongs to Me.' I'll step in and deal with your situation just to shut up the enemy." God likes shutting up the devil. Because He is holy and righteous, He hates evil, wickedness, sin, and pride.

Hannah prophesied about this very attribute of God that manifested in her situation. In verse 3 she prophesied to those who are proud and arrogant—the Peninnahs of the world. Hannah was speaking the word of the Lord, saying, "Talk no more so exceeding proudly; let not arrogancy come out of your mouth: for the LORD is a God of knowledge, and by him actions are weighed" (KJV). Because Peninnah had a few children, she thought she was somebody. She thought she was better than Hannah. She thought she was the best thing happening in her husband's life. But God saw her pride and the way she treated Hannah, and Hannah knew God would go before her to bring justice on her behalf. In verse 4 she declared, "The bows of the mighty men are broken" (KJV). In other words, God is a God who can break the power of the proud.

What's great about what Hannah was doing is that she was not only prophesying about her own situation. She was giving a word to generations to come. She was telling them that not only does God hate pride, arrogance, and when prideful and arrogant people put others down, but He is going to do something about it. When He sees those who stumble and are downtrodden, He comes and girds them with strength (v. 4). He will come and lift up the weak, frail, and depressed, those who are in a low place. And He is going to pull down the mighty.

Sometimes we've been down so long, we've been praying so long without any relief, that we beat ourselves up, thinking God doesn't love us. We feel that we are not the strong Christians we're supposed to be and that God is not pleased with us. When God sees us in that situation, His heart of mercy and compassion is moved to do something on our behalf. God heals the brokenhearted and lifts up the lowly. He looks out for those who are down, those who have no bread, and those who are weak. He says, "I will give you My strength."

God will lift you up when you can't lift yourself up. God hears your prayers. He hears your cries. He sees your situation. He has not forgotten about you. When it's all over, you will prophesy, just as Hannah did. God is going to open your mouth. Hannah went from praying inaudible prayers to prophesying. She had been in a place where she couldn't even find words to pray. Her lips just moved. But then in 1 Samuel 2 we find her boldly declaring the word of the Lord—and not just for her generation but for generations to come.

God will take you from a place where you aren't able to say anything; He will put His word in your mouth, and the word you prophesy will go forth to generation after generation. I am here to encourage you that despite what you are going through that is causing you to feel low and silenced, God will deliver you, and you will prophesy again. Do you believe it?

Your Samuel Is Coming Forth

Say this aloud: "My Samuel is coming forth." I hear the Lord saying, "I'm about to give some of you your Samuels. The prophetic is about to be birthed out of you. The prophetic is about to be released out of you." If you show me somebody who is or has been used mightily by God, I'll show you somebody who has been through something, somebody who has been mocked, talked about, and laughed at. They were not always on top, but God specializes in bringing people from the bottom. He hates pride and arrogance. Therefore He gives special grace to those who are down and lifts up the poor. This is why I love, worship, and praise Him. He is the same today, yesterday, and forever. If He blessed and delivered Hannah, He will bless and deliver you. Get your eyes off people and get your eyes on God. He has called you favor, so get ready as He brings your life in line with what He has named you. Your Samuel will come forth.

We learned five actions from Hannah—don't give up; fast; worship and weep; pray; and make a vow. In the next chapter and throughout the rest of this book, we are going to look at types of prayer and principles of prayer that break you out of desperate situations. We are going to break down the prayer component to give you more tools in your prayer arsenal as you get in position to see the power and blessing of God manifest in your life.

Prayers to Release the Blessing of Hannah

Father, I pray today that every Samuel that has been locked up in my womb be birthed in the name of Jesus. Open my womb, that I may not be barren or fruitless anymore.

I have been mocked and laughed at by the enemy. I've been made to feel ashamed. But I decree that today is my day for breakthrough.

Today is a day of birthing. Today my womb will be opened. Today my dream will come forth. My vision will come forth. My hope and desire will come forth. I prophesy it today in the name of Jesus.

I declare that my name is favor. My name is grace.

God is exalting me over the enemy. The enemy will no longer laugh at me and mock me. God will not let me be put to shame.

The same miracle that Hannah received will come forth unto me now in the name of Jesus.

I declare that I will have a Hannah-like breakthrough, and I will prophesy again.

Lord, I believe the words You have spoken to me. I will not live in a low place. I will live in a blessed place.

I am not cursed. I am blessed.

I will bring forth. I will not be barren. I will have children. I will multiply. I will be promoted. I will be exalted.

What the enemy meant for evil, You're turning around for my good.

I believe, Lord, that You are holy. You are righteous. You see my situation. I trust in You. You are my strength. You are my victory. You are my breakthrough.

I declare that everything I am meant to birth will come forth into its prophetic destiny.

The fruit of my womb is blessed.

Let my prayers birth a seed that will be extraordinary, unusual, different, holy, and prophetic.

I release my faith. I am blessed. I am prosperous.
God will do great things in my life.

My mouth will be enlarged over my enemies.

I will not be ashamed. I will not be a failure.

My name is favor. The favor of God is on my life. I will walk in the favor and grace of God in the days to come.

I believe that fruitfulness returns to
my life today in Jesus's name.

Chapter 2

When Desperation Becomes Your Friend

> In my desperation I prayed, and the LORD listened; he saved me from all my troubles.
>
> —PSALM 34:6, NLT

THERE ARE POINTS in a spiritual battle when it looks as though the enemy has had the final word. It looks like you will not make it. He's laughing at you. People you thought were friends and loved ones are laughing too. Coworkers and neighbors are saying, "I thought you were saved. I thought you went to church. I thought you went to that prophetic church. I thought you prophesy. How can I be doing better than you?" They're smoking hundred-dollar Cuban cigars, and you're trying to scrape together enough money for bus fare. Tell them, "Don't worry. Hold on. It's not over yet. You go ahead and talk, laugh, and think you have it made. Just wait, because I know God is about to do something in my life."

People may think that your holy living is a waste of time. They may question where your God is. But what they don't know—and you may not readily discern it either—is that you as a covenant believer will only be drawn in closer to God as a result of their mocking and torment. What they don't understand—and you may be coming into this revelation right now—is that they are driving you to pursue even harder all that God has for you. Torment and oppression and your all-out hunger for the power of God to manifest in your life will drive you to a place of weeping, crying, and desperation. We just saw this with Hannah.

It wouldn't seem to make sense from a natural perspective, but sometimes your lowest place is your best place. When it looks as if nobody cares, nobody tries to help you, nobody looks out for you, and it's just you and God, that is sometimes one of the best places to be. When everything and everyone is out of the picture and it is just you and God, this is the place where He can give you your Samuel. This is the moment when He can release to you not just a son but a Samuel. Your prayers will be heard, and the answer you receive will be of such supernatural proportions that it will exceed your every imagination. You will get to the point where you surrender and say:

> Now to Him who is able to do exceedingly abundantly beyond all that we ask or imagine.
>
> —EPHESIANS 3:20

God is saying, "You are praying for one thing that is within your level of understanding, but I'm about to release something greater in your life, something prophetic that will not only affect you now but will go out and affect your generation and those to come."

God allows some of the hardship we face to drive up the intensity of our pursuit, the intensity of our prayers, and the level of our faith and expectancy. God raises these levels because He wants to bring something out of us we never dreamed possible. Depending on people to be there for us in times when only God can make the difference will never work. There are some things man cannot do for us, and coming to this realization teaches us how to trust God. It teaches us how to draw near to Him.

This is the place of desperation I believe Hannah had come to, the place where her prayers no longer had words, the place where she was willing to do anything to receive what she needed from God. It is important that we dig deep into her process and examine the place of desperation she had come to and what was released into her life. Sometimes we just want answers to our problems or relief from our low place, but we don't want to go through what it takes to build the spiritual strength and maturity necessary to carry and then steward what we've prayed for.

This woman had no children, and she wanted a child more than anything. She kept praying and praying, and nothing changed. And this other woman kept mocking and mocking, and nothing changed. Hannah was shamed and ashamed. She felt hopeless, and then she became desperate. I believe this is when desperation becomes your friend.

Desperation Tears Down Barriers Between You and Your Promise

No one likes to be desperate, but it seems as if God looks upon desperate people. The woman in Luke 8:43–48 with an issue of blood was desperate. She was bleeding, which according to Jewish law meant that she was unclean. Year after year she had dealt with shame and rejection because of her condition. She was labeled and shunned by the community. She had no business being in a crowd. But she was so desperate after twelve years of hemorrhaging that she pressed through the crowd, touched the hem of Jesus' garment, and was healed. Because of the low place she had been reduced to, she developed a strong desire to remain in that place no longer. She got desperate and made a move that placed her at the feet of Jesus.

> But Jesus said, "Someone touched Me, for I perceive that power has gone out from Me."
>
> When the woman saw that she was not hidden, she came trembling. And falling down before Him, she declared to Him before all the people why she had touched Him and how she was healed immediately.
>
> Then He said to her, "Daughter, be of good cheer. Your faith has made you well. Go in peace."
>
> —LUKE 8:46–48

The woman's desperation forced her out of hiding, and she was met with compassion and healing. She was released back into life with the peace of God imparted to her. No more wrestling with the rejection of unanswered prayer. No more shame. No more labeling. No more mocking. With her healing came more than she imagined.

In Luke 5:17–26 there was a group of men who were desperate to get a lame man healed, but they couldn't get into the house where Jesus was ministering because it was crowded. Their desperation led them to climb on top of the roof of the house, break it open, and lower the man through the hole. Can you imagine what the owner of the house must have thought? "These folks are tearing up my house to get a healing!" But Jesus never rebuked them. The Bible says:

> When He saw their faith, He said to him, "Man, your sins are forgiven you."
>
> —LUKE 5:20

And to shut the mouths of the haters in the room—the Pharisees—Jesus took the man's healing from spiritual to physical, for those who needed a visual demonstration of how God sees the faith of the desperate:

> When Jesus perceived their thoughts, He answered them, "Why question in your hearts? Which is easier, to say, 'Your sins are forgiven you,' or to say, 'Rise up and walk'? But that you may know that the Son of Man has authority on earth to forgive sins," He said to the paralyzed man, "I say to you, rise, take up your bed, and go to your house." Immediately he rose before them, and took up that on which he lay, and departed to his own house, glorifying God.
>
> —LUKE 5:22–25

God is more concerned about you than a roof. You can always put a roof back together. So whatever the barrier is that stands between you and what God has promised, let desperation move you to tear it down.

Don't let people who don't know your story stop you from going after what you know God has promised. Imagine if Hannah would have listened to Peninnah and just given up, thinking it wasn't the will of God for her to have a child. What if she thought that was just the way things had to be, her waking up every day to affliction and mocking? What if she had given up? What if you give up? What if you listen to the people around you who say, "Get over it"?

Or maybe there are people around you who try to comfort you or get your attention off what you desire, like Hannah's husband, Elkanah, did: "Hannah, why are you weeping? And why do you not eat? Why is your heart grieved? Am I not better to you than ten sons?" (1 Sam. 1:8). Though he tried to comfort her by saying he loved her whether or not she could have children, his comfort wasn't enough. Even when they would go to the temple, Elkanah would give her a double portion of what he gave to his other wife, Peninnah, and all of her children. But when there is something you want from God and you know He wants it for you too, there is no substitute for that thing. The people around you who don't know your story, your inaudible groanings before the Lord day after day, month after month, and year after year—they will not understand your anguish. They will not understand your desperation.

But God sees and hears, and when you call upon His name in your desperation, He will not turn away from you. He will not try to divert your attention to something else. He will not say that you have gone overboard or that you are overreacting. God will honor His promise to you.

Desperation Moves You Closer to the Will of God

No one can teach you how to be desperate. This is not a strategy for getting what you want. What I am talking about in this chapter is harnessing certain positions, such as desperation, that come as a result of the attacks of the enemy and using them as catalysts to draw closer to God and closer to being aligned with His overall plan for your life. You cannot manipulate God. As I have already said, He sees, He hears, and He knows the intentions of every heart. But as believers we know that what the enemy has planned for our destruction can be turned around for our good. As a result of living life on this earth, at one time or another we will just find ourselves in desperate situations. We find ourselves in low places that make us feel as though we can't go on any longer with the way things are. But all things, even the dark and desperate moments, work toward our good. (See Romans 8:28.)

Now, this doesn't mean we should go looking to put ourselves in desperate situations just to get what we want from God. This will never go the way you think it will. Likewise, if you aren't careful, desperation can certainly lead to places outside of the will of God, and that is not what we want. If desperation causes you to act in a way that takes you further from God's favor and further from righteousness and the presence of God, you are putting yourself in a position to be given over to all kinds of torment. What I am saying is, we can learn to let desperation give us razor-sharp focus on the thing *He* has promised and ordained for us. We can harness desperation so it will cause us to do whatever we need to do to get our lives in line with God so He will be moved to rescue and deliver us.

Desperate people do desperate things. But whatever you do, allow the Spirit of God to guide you as you pursue healing, peace, fulfillment, fruitfulness, favor, destiny, blessing, or purpose.

Desperation Forces You to Make a Vow

As desperation draws you closer to God and His will, it will cause you to realize that what He is preparing to give you isn't just for you. Desperation will cause you to pray prayers such as "Nevertheless not My will, but Yours, be done" (Luke 22:42). Desperation will cause you to offer back to God the thing He is promising to give you. This is the powerful change of heart that God was aiming for. You go from thinking about how the promise will fulfill you to how it will bless God and His people. We see this change in Hannah. First Samuel 1:10–11 says:

> And she was bitter, and prayed to the LORD, and wept severely. So she made a vow and said, "O LORD of Hosts, if You will indeed look on the affliction of Your maidservant, and remember me and not forget Your maidservant, but will give to Your maidservant a baby boy, then I will give him to the LORD all the days of his life, and no razor shall touch his head."

She had become so desperate that she was willing to give her son back to God in service. She wanted him to be brought into the world so badly that she was willing to surrender him to God if that meant he could be born. "Just open my womb, God," she cried out. "Just give me a son. I don't even want him for myself. I'll dedicate him to You." And Samuel was born.

Now hear this. This is what I believe God was saying to Hannah as He honored her request: "Not only am I going to give you a son, but I am also going to make sure your son goes down in the record of history as one of the greatest prophets Israel has ever had. Not only will he go down in history, but the story of your prayers and deliverance will end up in Scripture. You will be known not as a barren woman but as a woman who was highly favored. You will live out the fullness of your calling as Hannah, the favored one."

This is the power of making a vow to the Lord. Desperation will have us looking for all available options, all open doors: "What do I need to do? What do I need to pray? Is my heart right? Do you need to change something about me first? What is it, God? Show me. I am desperate!" Then when He shows us that it is all about Him, we will find ourselves surrendering back to God the very things we wanted, because we recognize that our desires are centered in Him in the first place.

As we delight in Him, He will give us the desires of our hearts (Ps. 37:4). It's interesting that the word *delight* in this verse means "to be soft or pliable."[1] Delighting in God is not so much about taking pleasure in Him as it is about your becoming soft and pliable in His hands so that you are able to be shaped and molded by Him.

Times of desperation soften us to the leading of the Lord. Through the process of waiting for an answer to prayer, our hearts begin to change, and we start to want what He wants. His desire becomes our desire. At the time of Hannah's situation, God needed to reconnect with His people. If you read 1 Samuel 3, you learn that the word of the Lord was "rare in those days. There was no vision coming forth" (v. 1). There was a prophetic drought in the land. And then there's Hannah, who wanted a son. God saw an opportunity to bless her and restore the prophetic mantle in Israel. Through her process she became softened to discern God's desire to have a prophet who would be true to Him. Her prayer became a vow that was in line with God's desire.

When your prayers become vows back to God to bless Him with what He gives you, you have arrived at the place where breakthrough is inevitable.

Desperation Is the Final Step Before Breakthrough

When it looks like you are at your lowest point, that's when you're on the verge of your greatest miracle. Think about this: Hannah had been desperate for a child for so long, but she made a vow to give him back to God. Then when she got the child, she kept her vow. She raised him until he was weaned and then delivered him to Eli the priest. The Bible says:

> When she had weaned him, she took him up with her with three bulls, one ephah of flour, and a bottle of wine. And she brought him to the house of the Lord in Shiloh, though the boy was young. Then they slaughtered a bull, and they brought the boy to Eli. And she said, "Oh, my lord! As you live, my lord, I am the woman that stood by you here praying to the Lord. For this boy I prayed, and the Lord has given me my petition which I asked of Him. Therefore also I have let the Lord have him. As long as he lives he will be dedicated to the Lord." And he worshipped the Lord there.
>
> —1 Samuel 1:24–28

Though it seems like this is the perfect ending to Hannah's story, it was only the beginning of her breakthrough. Hannah ended up having five more children (1 Sam. 2:21). She went from crying to rejoicing. She went from barrenness to fruitfulness.

Your days of weeping are also over. It doesn't matter how much you've cried or how long the devil has tormented you; it's over. When you call on the Lord and allow desperation to become part of His perfect work in your life, you will get what you have prayed for. God will step into your situation and open up your womb. I'm not only talking about having natural babies. I am also talking about spiritual barrenness being broken off your life. Perhaps you are in a place where it seems as though you can't bring forth your destiny, purpose, dream, or vision. You've been pregnant with potential and with the promises of an abundant and prosperous life, but you can't get it out. As you begin to pray desperate prayers, and as desperation leads you to a vow of surrender and obedience, your womb will open up.

Prayers of the Desperate

I am desperate, and my desperation drives me to the throne of God. I declare that my prayers are answered. My miracle is coming forth.

I pray in desperation, and the Lord hears. He will deliver me from all my troubles (Ps. 34:6).

May Your mercy come quickly to meet me. I am in desperate need (Ps. 79:8).

Hear my cry and rescue me from those who pursue me. I am in desperate need (Ps. 142:6).

In my trouble, Lord, I turn to You. In desperation, I seek You and will find You (2 Chron. 15:4).

In my desperation, God is my refuge, high tower, and stronghold (Ps. 9:9).

I am in trouble. I am desperate. Lord, do not stand far off. Do not hide Yourself from me (Ps. 10:1).

O Lord my God, answer my desperate prayer (1 Kings 8:28; 2 Chron. 6:19).

From my youth I have been afflicted and near death. I am desperate. Do not reject me. Do not hide Your face from me (Ps. 88:14–15).

Thank You, Lord, for springing into action on my behalf. Thank You for providing me the safety I so desperately desire (Ps. 12:5).

Lord, I seek You in the day of my trouble. I desperately require You. In the night I stretch my hand out to You in prayer (Ps. 77:2).

I desperately long for Your deliverance. I find hope in Your Word (Ps. 119:81).

Chapter 3

The Power of Persevering Prayer

> Rejoice in hope, be patient in suffering, persevere in prayer.
>
> —Romans 12:12

One of the greatest keys to breaking through desperate times and receiving miracles and consistent advances in your life is to persevere in prayer. Hannah persevered in prayer, which we saw when year after year she put her petition for a son before the Lord. Persevering prayer is the kind of prayer many believers don't understand because they want to pray one time and see things change immediately. If something doesn't change the way they think it will, then they just give up.

In the key verse for this chapter, notice the context within which we are being commanded to persevere in prayer. The Book of Romans is all about suffering and tribulation, because the church at that particular time was going through a tremendous amount of persecution. From the time when the Acts of the Apostles were written to the time when the majority of the Epistles were written, there was a shift happening. It is sometimes referred to as the end of the age or the end of the world, which was the end of the old covenant world or old covenant system.

The religious system that opposed the teachings of the apostles was part of the old covenant system that did not believe Jesus was the Son of God and considered the followers of Christ to be heretics. They considered Christianity to be a false religion. They considered Christ to be a false prophet and a heretic. Because of this, the church experienced a great amount of suffering, trials, tribulations, and persecution from the old covenant religious system. But the more they fought the church, the more it grew. So these Christians were living in a desperate time full of testing and trials, and they had to persevere.

The implication is this: when we are going through a season of trial or testing or a difficult season of intense pressure, one of the things God admonishes us to do is to pray. The Bible says, "Is any among you afflicted? let him pray. Is any merry? let him sing psalms" (James 5:13, KJV). So if you are afflicted or suffering, pray. If you're going through something, pray. Prayer is the key to overcoming any kind of affliction, test, or trial. The worst thing you can do is to become discouraged and stop praying. The worst thing that can happen is that you give up and just allow things to happen without asking God to intervene and deliver you.

Looking back at the verse at the beginning of this chapter, in the King James Version it says that we should be "patient in tribulation; *continuing instant in prayer*" (Rom. 12:12, emphasis added). I looked up the phrase *continuing instant* in different Bible versions, and here is how some of them translated it:

- "Busy in prayer" (WYC).
- "Persevere in prayer" (MEV). To *persevere* means you don't give up. You don't throw in the towel. You keep going despite what you're going through.
- "Faithful in prayer" (NIV). Be committed and faithful to a life of prayer.
- "Devote yourselves to prayer" (CEB). *Devote* means "to commit by a solemn act" or "to give over or direct (time, money, effort, etc.) to a cause, enterprise, or activity."[1]
- "Never stop praying" (CEV).
- "Pray all the time" (ERV).
- "Pray continually" (GW).
- "Be persistent in prayer" (CSB).

This verse, then, provides a picture of someone who is going through something in life but is persistent, consistent, devoted, steadfast, faithful, persevering, and busy. He doesn't give up. He doesn't become slothful and lazy when it comes to prayer.

When many of us go through desperate times in our lives, our prayer life becomes less consistent, even though this is the very thing that will give us the strength to overcome the pressures, trials, and tests. For some, remaining persistent in prayer is a challenge. Sometimes when things are going badly, there is a tendency to want to sleep. Have you ever wanted to sleep through your problems? When you are asleep—whether physically or spiritually—you're not dealing with anything. But Romans 12:12 is suggesting that we do the opposite. Instead of decreasing our prayer life or sleeping, we need to stay awake in the spirit and pray. Notice what Jesus said when He and His disciples came to the Garden of Gethsemane:

> "My soul is very sorrowful, even to death. Wait here, and keep watch with Me."
>
> He went a little farther, and falling on His face, He prayed, "O My Father, if it is possible, let this cup pass from Me. Nevertheless, not as I will, but as You will."
>
> Then He came to the disciples and found them sleeping, and said to Peter, "So, could you not keep watch with Me one hour?"
>
> —MATTHEW 26:38–40

Jesus was praying so hard in the garden that His body began to release great amounts of sweat and perspiration. The Bible says that "His sweat became like great drops of blood falling down to the ground" (Luke 22:44). So it was not a time to sleep. It was not a time to be lazy. It was a time to really press and persevere.

Persevering prayer is not a regular, everyday type of prayer. It is the kind of prayer you pray in times of emergency. Whether it's financial, physical, spiritual, or an attack of hell on your city, there are seasons of desperation when you really need to understand and utilize the power of persevering prayer. When a believer or a group of believers prays through a difficult season on a consistent basis, it's only a matter of time before supernatural breakthroughs and answers come and desperate situations turn around.

God would never ask us to do something unless there would be some benefit in doing it, and prayer is not some religious exercise that you do just to make yourself feel better. There must be some reason the Scriptures tell us to be instant and continue in prayer. Evidently this type of praying is what you need at certain times in your life. There's simply no substitute for this kind of praying.

Now, we know there is the prayer of faith, the prayer of agreement, the prayer of consecration, praying in the Spirit, praying in tongues, and other kinds of prayer—some of which we are discussing in this book. But persevering prayer doesn't give up. It is the kind of action in prayer that keeps us praying and praying, in season and out of season.

Times of great testing and tribulation are designed by the enemy to destroy you, break you down, and cause you to become so discouraged and depressed that you can't enjoy life, that you want to give up on life altogether. The fear they bring into your life can paralyze and overwhelm you to the point that you are ineffective in doing what God has called you to do. Testing and trials even affect the way you live, so you can't even live your life in a consistent way. You can find yourself getting physically sick and emotionally imbalanced, becoming double-minded and confused. You can find yourself battling all kinds of issues and getting angry and upset, withdrawing from life and cutting off relationships with people.

It has never been the will of God for you to be defeated. God's will for you includes your being strong and stable enough to rise up in prayer when trouble comes. His will for you is to be led by His Spirit to persevere in prayer for as long as the battle wages, day after day, week after week, and month after month. He wants you to pray until you break through what the enemy has designed for your life.

Learn to Be Instant in Prayer

We've looked at various ways different Bible versions describe persevering prayer. I like the description that includes the word *instant*. It gives the feeling of spontaneity. There's no set time or place that you pray prayers like this. You can pray them at any time and anywhere, whenever the Spirit of God stirs you. You can pray in your closet, in your car when you're driving to work, before you eat or go to sleep, and when you get up in the morning. It can just be something that stirs up on the inside of you, and you begin to pray and ask God for deliverance from the things that are coming against your life.

This prayer is made available to you so that you don't end up a casualty. Too many people end up being casualties because they let the devil roll over them. They have the attitude that whatever comes must be God's will. They just lie down and let it happen instead of being instant in persevering prayer. This constant prayer, this praying without ceasing, this praying all the time, this praying when you're dealing with things can turn the tide in a spiritual battle.

Many people simply don't know how to pray. We live in a society where people do a lot of talking about God, but it's very seldom that you find someone who really knows how to talk to God. Then when the challenges of life come, they don't know how to deal with them. They cry, weep, complain, murmur, get depressed, blame everybody, get angry, and then they get sick. They do everything but remain constant in prayer.

Listen, whatever weapons the enemy forms against your life, if you are a believer, you have authority to stand against them. Don't just lie down and allow anything to come into your life. If it's sickness and disease, learn how to stand up and say, "Devil, no! I refuse that. I am a child of God. By His stripes I am healed. I'm not going to accept everything that comes my way." Learn to resist the devil. Have enough strength in your spirit to say, "No. By faith I rebuke that. I don't care if it's been in my family. I don't care if it's been in my generational bloodline. No. I'm a child of God. I'm redeemed by the blood of the Lamb."

Now, it's OK to have people pray for you or to ask somebody to agree with you in prayer. But you should also learn how to pray for yourself. Here is how you do that:

1. Get around people who know how to pray. Get to a church where Spirit-filled and prophetic prayer and intercession are part of the culture. You can learn to pray or be strengthened in prayer when you see others do it.

2. Study the Word of God. Learn how to pray according to the Word of God. Much of what led me to write my Prayers for Spiritual Battle series came from the Lord leading me to pray the Scriptures as a means of spiritual warfare.

3. Be filled with the Holy Spirit with the evidence of speaking in tongues. If you don't know anything else, learn how to pray in the Spirit. Pray in tongues. Pray in the Holy Ghost when you don't know what to pray for. Romans 8:26 says, "Likewise, the Spirit helps us in our weaknesses, for we do not know what to pray for as we ought, but the Spirit Himself intercedes for us with groanings too deep for words."

We all go through things in life that demand that we know how to pray without ceasing. This kind of prayer is powerful because it strengthens us in long seasons of desperation.

It also needs to be said here that if it seems as though you're always in a desperate position, it may not be the devil attacking you. It may be that you've been making bad decisions that have put you in bad situations. There are hard times that come as a result of foolishness or disobedience, and I really do worry about people who are always going through something. The Christian life is one of victory. These are not the desperate times and desperate prayers I am talking about in this book. I am mainly talking about praying through the times when you are doing what is right, you're living clean, yet you find yourself going through a testing season. There is a whole other teaching that will help if you find yourself doing things that have put you in bad situations.[2]

Persevering Prayer Strengthens You for Long War

> The struggle between the house of Saul and the house of David endured, but David grew stronger as Saul became weaker.
>
> —2 SAMUEL 3:1

One thing that demons cannot stand is when you keep putting pressure on them through consistent prayer. The enemy starts strong, fixing his weapons for a quick battle. He wants to come into the ring, knock you out, and walk away. His strategy is not built for a twelve-round match. His plan is to get in and get out. But with persevering prayer in your spiritual arsenal, you can tell the devil, "I'm a twelve-rounder. You aren't going to knock me out in the first round. This fight is going the distance."

If you know anything about boxing, then you know winning the fight is not all about the head shots. It's those body shots delivered consistently over the length of the fight that can do the most damage. Persisting in prayer through seasons of affliction is just like delivering a fury of jabs to the enemy's midsection. If you keep sticking him right there in the body, then his arms start coming down and his head is exposed and unprotected. *Then* you can get those head shots. This is one good thing about growing up in the hood: you learn a little bit about fighting.

Almost everyone can remember how Mike Tyson used to come out in the first round and—BAM!—his opponent would be laid out in the boxing ring, knocked out cold from one of his deadly punches. But then Mike Tyson fought Buster Douglas. Mike flew to Japan and didn't prepare.

Why should he have? His plan was to knock Buster out. He had a record for knocking people out with one punch. Why would this time be any different?

But Buster had in his mind that he wasn't going out like that. I will never forget this fight. Buster had tassels on his shoes, and I think his mother had just passed, so he was mad. Buster got tangled up with Mike, and Mike couldn't knock him out that first round. They kept going, and the longer it went, the more Mike was in trouble, because again, all he planned for was a knockout in the first round. Finally Buster got in there, measured Mike up, hit him one time, and then—BAM!—Mike went down. Though Mike won other fights, his career never fully rebounded. Sometime after this fight there were reports of him biting another fighter's ear. He just wasn't the same.

Long fights confuse the enemy and upset his strategies. "Thrilla in Manila" was a historic heavyweight championship fight between Joe Frazier and Muhammad Ali, where after fourteen rounds both men were ready to quit. It was one hundred-something degrees in Manila at the time of the fight. I've been to Manila; it is hot and very humid, and you just sweat. At the end of the fourteenth round Ali commented that it was the hardest fight of his life and he felt like giving up. Reports say he told his corner to cut his gloves off, but they ignored him.[3] The men wore each other down until Joe Frazier's corner stopped the fight after the fourteenth round.[4]

This is what you do in prayer: you wear the enemy down and you keep praying. You may start off feeling weak, but the more you pray, the stronger you feel. The more you pray, the more you're charged up. You may start off thinking you can't win, but keep praying. Keep praying. Keep praying. All of a sudden you will feel joy coming and strength coming. At the same time the enemy is going to get weaker and weaker.

In the long war between David and Saul, the Bible says that David got stronger and stronger, and Saul got weaker and weaker, until eventually David won, Saul was killed, and David became king of Israel.

We don't like long wars. We want a quick end. But sometimes things take a little longer. This is where God's Word encourages us to be patient in tribulation and persistent in prayer. We will soon learn that if we keep praying and keep the pressure on, it's only a matter of time before breakthrough will come.

Persevering Prayer Is Not for the Faint

Persisting in prayer through some of life's darkest hours is not for the faint of heart. It's not for those who need things to happen how and when they want them to, and if things don't turn out like that, they're out. Persevering prayer is for the Hannahs, the people who have been pursuing their healing and have never given up, for those who are willing to break open rooftops, and for those who are willing to go all twelve rounds.

I'm talking about saints who know how to press and pray through stuff, saints who know when and how to pray and won't give up, even when it looks bad. They don't go by how things look. They walk by faith and not by sight, because in the natural it could look like things are getting worse instead of better. But saints have learned how not to pay attention to what a situation looks like. They know that God is in heaven and He hears their prayers. They are confident He will do something about their situation and that it's only a matter of time before they see breakthrough.

People of God, I implore you: Keep praying. Keep interceding. Be constant and persevere. Pray continually. Persist. Never stop. Devote yourself. Remain steadfast, instant, and faithful. Instead of being a busybody, be busy in prayer. If you can be a busybody and talk to everyone you know, you can take that same energy and pray. Persevering prayer is talking to God and, instead of getting anxious and giving in to fear and worry, continually bringing your petitions to Him.

Pray through whatever comes to steal, kill, or destroy the things that God has set aside for you. Pray through a storm, hurricane, tsunami, and earthquake. Pray through all of the devices of the enemy. If you have to get all by yourself where nobody is clapping or cheering and there is no keyboard behind you or mic in your hand, do it. You will come through with a testimony. And not the same ones you've read about—Shadrach, Meshach, and Abednego, and others. You will come through with your own testimony, what God did for you. I'm telling you now, you'll come out on the other side with more than you had before the enemy attacked you. God gave Job twice as much as he'd had before the attack came. Hannah came out with five children more than the one she prayed for.

Don't be a spiritual wimp. The devil is nothing but a bully. Take a stand against his attacks on your life. Refuse to let him walk all over you. Refuse to lie down and let him do whatever he wants to do and then cower in a corner feeling sorry for yourself. One of the worst things you can do is to allow yourself to be overcome with self-pity. Jesus came that you might have life and have it more abundantly (John 10:10). Sinners should not be enjoying life more than saints. We are children of God.

We've discovered that persistent and persevering prayer is not an instant spiritual potion that, when applied, yields instant results. Breakthrough may take some time, but I challenge you to add this weapon of prayer to your arsenal. Allow it to build within you a formidable strength that the enemy will not be able to overpower easily. Commit to keep on praying until every mountain, every Goliath, every obstacle, every enemy, every hater, every devil, every attack, every plan, every strategy, and every plot of hell against your life is brought to nothing.

Declarations to Persevere in Prayer

Lord, I believe in the power of prayer.

I believe that no weapon formed against me will prosper (Isa. 54:17).

I believe that He who is in me is greater than he who is in the world (1 John 4:4).

Father, I will not be discouraged, and I will not give up. I will pray through every situation, every test, every trial, and every attack of hell.

I rededicate and recommit myself to prayer, in the name of Jesus.

Lord, I believe that You are a miracle-working God and that You are the God of the breakthrough.

Lord, I lift my hands to You and pray that everything that is attacking my life, everything that has been sent by the enemy, be overcome by Your hand and by Your power.

Lord, I pray and I thank You for deliverance. I thank You for breakthrough. I thank You for miracles. I thank You for signs and wonders.

I thank You, Lord, for bringing me through and causing me to overcome every assignment of hell, in the name of Jesus.

Lord, I thank You for helping me stand. I will not be knocked down. I am getting stronger and stronger, and as I persevere in prayer the enemy is getting weaker and weaker.

Father, I thank You for being my battle axe and weapons of war (Jer. 51:20).

I will not give up in prayer. I will not give up praying for my city. I will not give up praying for my nation. I will not give up praying for my church. I will not give up praying for my community. I will not give up praying for my family. I will remain instant in prayer. I will keep praying and praying until revival, glory, and breakthrough come.

I believe in the power of persistent, persevering, and constant prayer.

I release my burden for prayer. Every assignment against my life will be defeated in the name of Jesus.

Chapter 4

Crossing Over

> In the morning Joshua got up early; then he and all the children of Israel set out from Shittim and came to the Jordan. They stayed there before crossing over.
>
> —JOSHUA 3:1

COMING FROM A place of desperation, affliction, torment, testing, and trial and crossing into a place of peace, healing, blessing, favor, and prosperity requires faith and the presence of God. One of the keys to Hannah's breakthrough was that she sought the presence of God. She went to the house of the Lord to pray. It doesn't appear from her story that she attempted to work things out on her own. If you can recall the stories of other barren women in the Bible—Sarah and Rachel, for example—you will notice that they didn't pursue God's presence as they sought the thing they wanted most. Instead they took matters into their own hands and first produced Ishmaels instead of Isaacs, Dans instead of Josephs. Because Hannah remained in God's presence, she got it right the first time and delivered Samuel. Other examples from men and women of God follow a similar pattern.

When God commanded Moses to take the people of

Israel from the wilderness into a land flowing with milk and honey, Moses wasn't even impressed with the blessing on the other side because God said He wasn't going with them. (See Exodus 33:3.) Instead He pleaded with God: "If Your Presence does not go with us, do not bring us up from here. For how will it be known that I have found favor in Your sight, I and Your people? Is it not by Your going with us, so that we will be distinguished, I and Your people, from all the people who are on the face of the earth?" Of course, God granted Moses' request.

We see the same thing in the life of David. He was blessed because no matter what tragedy or triumph he experienced, he held on to the presence of God. For David, his life depended on it.

In the last chapter we looked at how persevering in prayer breaks us out of the desperate place. Now we are going to use the story of how Joshua and the children of Israel were finally able to cross over into the Promised Land as a template for how we can cross over from our place of desperation and affliction into a place of favor, blessing, and prosperity.

One of the major points in their story that we will focus on is that in getting our breakthrough, we cannot forget to take God with us into that next place. Like Moses said, the blessing isn't worth it if we lose the anointing, glory, and presence of God on our way out. He can take everything except His presence, because if we have His presence, we can get everything else back. With God's presence you have victory and joy and can defeat the enemy. I want you to get in the mentality that although you desire to be delivered, there is no substitute for God Himself.

His presence is the one thing you need in your life to cross over into breakthrough—from a place of barrenness to a place of fruitfulness and blessing. You cannot cross over without it. If you lost the presence, you need to do whatever it takes to get it back. If you have sin in your life, you need to get rid of it. If you have something in your life that grieves the Holy Spirit and you don't feel God's presence, allow Him to search your heart. You need His presence in your life if you want to be blessed.

Step Into the River

Joshua chapter 3 is the story of Joshua and Israel crossing the Jordan to go into the land of promise. This is the Israelites' second crossover, really, because they had already crossed over the Red Sea coming out of Egypt. (See Exodus 14.) God had delivered Israel from slavery and destroyed Pharaoh. God had set them free and made plans for them to possess Canaan and claim it as their Promised Land. (See Exodus 6:7–8.) But as they crossed over, they first had to go through the wilderness and conquer a few enemies. This is where they lost perspective. They murmured and complained until God passed judgment on them, saying that none of them would see the Promised Land and that they would all die in the wilderness because of their unbelief. (See Deuteronomy 1:26–40; Hebrews 3:18–19.)

The only two individuals who would cross over were Caleb and Joshua, who had to wait forty years until everyone in the unbelieving generation died before they could go over and possess the land. They were the only two of that generation to cross over, because they believed God. Let me tell you, you can die in your desperate place—your wilderness—because you won't believe God for His promises. Can you imagine?

So this is where we find Joshua in Joshua 3. He led Israel to the Jordan River, they camped there for three days, and now in verses 14 and 15 we read that they are about to cross over into the Promised Land, except that the Jordan River was overflowing its banks. It had become a mighty, rushing river because of the spring rains. The question became, How would more than a million people cross this rushing river and get to the other side?

They were right there. They could probably see the Promised Land from where they stood, but something seemingly impossible to cross blocked their way. Let's look at what God does.

> They commanded the people, "When you see the ark of the covenant of the LORD your God and the Levite priests carrying it, then you shall set out from where you are and go behind it."...
>
> And Joshua said, "By this you will know that the living God is among you, and that He will thoroughly drive out the Canaanites, the Hittites, the Hivites, the Perizzites, the Girgashites, the Amorites, and the Jebusites from before you. See, the ark of the covenant of the LORD of all the earth is passing before you into the Jordan. Now select twelve men from the tribes of Israel, one man per tribe. When the soles of the feet of the priests who bear the ark of the LORD, the Lord of all the earth, touch the water of the Jordan, the water of the

> Jordan that flows from upstream will be cut off and pile up."
>
> —Joshua 3:3, 10–13

The emphasis here is that through Joshua, God told Israel that He wanted the priests and leaders to separate themselves from the rest of the people. He wanted them to go before the people with the ark of God—the ark of the covenant. And, by faith, they would have to step into that river. They didn't know how deep the river was. They didn't know if they would make it to the other side. But God had commanded them to take the ark, put their feet in the water, and proceed across the river. When they put their feet in the water, the Bible says that God intervened, caused the stream to stop, and opened a way for them to carry the ark across the river. This also made a way for the people to cross after them.

> When the carriers of the ark came to the Jordan, the feet of the priests carrying the ark dipped into the edge of the water. (Now the Jordan overflows its banks all the days of the harvest.) Then the water that flows down from upstream stood still and rose up in a heap very far away at Adam, the city beside Zarethan. The water that flows down toward the Sea of Arabah (the Dead Sea) stopped and was cut off. The people crossed over opposite Jericho. The priests carrying the ark of the covenant of the Lord stood firmly on dry ground in the middle of the Jordan, and all Israel crossed over on dry ground *until the entire people completed crossing over* the Jordan.
>
> —Joshua 3:15–17, emphasis added

We are seeing here that God will supernaturally intervene in your time of desperation and will make a way for you to cross over—completely. In other words, you will not cross over *completely* without God's help.

Now, the ark of the covenant, of course, is the box that God commanded Moses to make (Exod. 37). It represents the presence and glory of God, sometimes referred to as His shekinah. Whoever had the ark carried with them the presence of God. Israel was the only nation that had possession of this ark. And this ark, which represented the presence of God, opened the way for them to cross over into the Promised Land.

The message here is very simple: you need God's presence in your life in order to cross over from your place of desperation to your Promised Land. There is a river flowing right in front of you that you must have the faith to step into. Whether it's too deep or flowing too hard and fast, nothing should hinder you from putting your faith in the word of the Lord over your life and stepping into that river. What He does next is supernatural. He will stop the flow and reverse the flow of the river so you cross over to the other side. Anything coming at you, anything that had been rushing toward you to knock you off your feet and carry you away, will be stopped and reversed. But you must have the presence of God with you.

One of the things I like about this story is how Joshua prophesied the victories God would give Israel once they crossed over: "He will thoroughly drive out the Canaanites, the Hittites, the Hivites, the Perizzites, the Girgashites, the Amorites, and the Jebusites from before you" (Josh. 3:10). God is going to drive your enemies out of your Promised

Land. They will not ravage the promises and blessings God has set aside for you. After you cross over, His promises are yes and amen. Your Peninnahs, your Leahs, and your Hagars will be thoroughly driven out. You will cross over to possess your promise. But you can't cross over without God's presence. Let's talk about how to get it back if you lost it, and how to stir it up if you know He's there.

Capture the Presence of God

What we need to see in this story of Joshua and the Israelites is that there was a whole new generation who believed God standing at the bank of this river. The old generation of doubters and complainers had died in the wilderness. I want you to look at this prophetic word and hear what God is speaking to you. If you allow it, the wilderness can be a place where all of you dies, or it can be a place where the part of you that needs to die dies and the part of you that needs to live is made alive. We'll talk about this more in a later chapter, but I mention it here because we need to understand the wilderness can be a place of discovery or of great loss.

Sometimes we are in the wilderness so long that we lose some of our fight. We lose some of the fire of the presence of God and of His anointing. Have you ever been in a place like this? You've been beaten down so much that it is hard to feel that God is with you. When you go to church, you don't feel the anointing, you don't feel joy, and you don't feel the presence of God. You just kind of stand and watch everybody else praise God, but your hand never goes up. You don't feel anything. You may have lost the presence of

God. My encouragement to you is this: You'd better get it back before you try to go any further. You need His presence if you want to be blessed.

I know we've been taught not to depend on feelings so much, but I believe God wants us to feel that He is with us. And we know that God is always faithful to His promises when He says, "I will be with you. I will not abandon you. I will not leave you" (Josh. 1:5), or "I am with you always, even to the end" (Matt. 28:20). We can count on these promises—and sometimes praying through them and thanking Him for His presence causes us to *feel* that He is with us. It is reassuring.

I don't know how people go for long periods without feeling that God is with them in a powerful and manifest way. I don't want to just know His presence; I want His shekinah—His tangible, manifest presence—to be with me. Here's how to stir it up.

Ask the Holy Spirit to search and purify your heart.

> Search me, O God, and know my heart: try me, and know my thoughts: And see if there be any wicked way in me, and lead me in the way everlasting.
>
> —Psalm 139:23–24, kjv

Sin, rejection, rebellion, bitterness, unbelief, and perversion—all of these separate us from God. As we learned, a whole generation of people died in the wilderness and did not get to take hold of the promises of God because they did not believe God.

Ask God to show you what may be separating you from Him. If you have sin in your life, you need to get rid of it.

If you have something that grieves the Holy Ghost and you don't feel God's presence, ask God to show you what it is. Then repent and be delivered.

Take time for praise and worship.

> But You are holy, O You who inhabits the praises of Israel.
>
> —Psalm 22:3

This word *inhabits* is the Greek word *yashab.* It means "to dwell, remain, sit, abide; to be set; [to] have one's abode."[1] It means "to occupy as a place of settled residence or habitat."[2] In other words, God abides in our praise. He remains in our praise. He stays in or occupies our praise as if it is His residence or dwelling place. Our praise is God's habitat. So if you want God's presence to abide and dwell with you, open your mouth and praise Him.

Begin to tell Him of His greatness. Recount past victories and how He has brought you out. If you don't know what to say, get into the psalms of David, Heman, and Asaph. They were men who knew how to laud the praises of the Lord continually until His glory fell. Remind yourself of His promise to never leave you nor forsake you. Jump and shout it out with a loud voice. Don't stop until the glory comes.

Pray, and be prayed for.

> The Lord is near to all those who call upon Him, to all who call upon Him in truth.
>
> —Psalm 145:18

God's ear is inclined or bent toward His people. When we pray, He hears us. He is near to us when we call on Him.

There are many ways to approach God. One scripture says to approach Him boldly and receive help in times of need (Heb. 4:16). Another encourages us to pray with all kinds of prayer (Eph. 6:18). Still another says to pray without ceasing (1 Thess. 5:17). We are learning even now about various prayers to pray in desperate times.

Speak in tongues. Pray in the Spirit. Bow low before the Lord. Let someone pray for you and lay hands on you to stir up God's Spirit that is within you (2 Tim. 1:6–7). Where God's Spirit is, His presence is there also. Be eager to seek God and ask Him to fill you. He said that those who seek Him will find Him (Jer. 29:13).

Get to a church that stirs up the glory of God.

> When the priests came out from the Most Holy Place—for all the priests who were present had consecrated themselves, without keeping separate divisions—and all the Levitical singers, Asaph, Heman, and Jeduthun, with their sons and relatives, all clothed in fine linen, with cymbals, harps, and lyres, stood to the east of the altar, and with them one hundred twenty priests who were sounding with trumpets, it happened, when the trumpet players and singers made one sound to praise and give thanks to the Lord, and when they lifted up their voice with the trumpets and cymbals and all the instruments of music and praised the Lord saying, "For He is good and His mercy endures forever," that the house, the house of the Lord, was filled with a cloud. And the priests were not able

> to stand in order to serve because of the cloud, for the glory of the LORD had filled the house of God.
>
> —2 CHRONICLES 5:11–14

We've already discussed the temple of God being the place of God's presence. But when we gather together in the house of the Lord with pure and consecrated hearts, lifting up prayer and worship and releasing the word of the Lord, His presence will descend on us like a cloud. I'm sorry, people of God, I'm not going to a church where I cannot feel any anointing and there is no glory. I know we walk by faith and not by sight, but as I said previously, I have to feel the glory and the anointing of God. His presence brings joy, and the joy of the Lord is my strength. We need God's glory in our lives. We need His presence, and it can come down on us like a cloud when we gather in His house to worship Him.

Take a step of faith and just obey God.

> Peter answered Him and said, "Lord, if it is You, bid me come to You on the water."
>
> He said, "Come."
>
> And when Peter got out of the boat, he walked on the water to go to Jesus.
>
> —MATTHEW 14:28–29

Peter stepped out of the boat, and Jesus was there with him, enabling him to do the impossible. Peter walked on water because he trusted God more than he trusted what he thought was possible. He saw Jesus there—God's presence made flesh, the ark of God—and he stepped out of the boat.

Can you imagine being Peter or one of the Israelite priests at the bank of the river? They stepped out into the water just obeying God, not knowing what was going to happen. They had never done anything like that before. What God did in both stories had never happened before.

Sometimes you may have to take a step of faith and just obey God. You have to step out. The priests stepped in the water, and all of a sudden the river began to open up. God made a way for a whole nation to cross over.

Be humble.

> Humble yourselves in the sight of the Lord, and He will lift you up.
>
> —James 4:10

> God resists the proud, but gives grace to the humble.
>
> —James 4:6

> He has concern for the lowly, but the proud one He knows from a distance.
>
> —Psalm 138:6

God honors humility. He hears the cries of the humble and gives them His grace, which is a manifestation of His presence. He resists and stays far from the proud. If you want God's presence in your life, be humble.

Stay close to Jesus.

> They woke Him and said, "Teacher, do You not care that we are perishing?" He rose and rebuked the

> wind, and said to the sea, "Peace, be still!" Then the wind ceased and there was a great calm.
>
> —Mark 4:38–39

In the spirit realm, you will never need to wake Jesus up. He has ascended to heaven and is now at the right hand of His Father (Eph. 1:20). Therefore, in His glorified state, He never sleeps (Ps. 121:4). But being able to reach out to Him and have His presence with you through the storms of life brings peace and calm. He calms the storm so that you can cross over to the other side in peace.

Jesus is the ark. He is the presence of God made flesh. As a gift of salvation, of receiving Jesus's sacrifice on the cross, we have access to the unveiled presence of God. We are able to boldly approach God because of what Jesus did. Accepting Him into our hearts means that He is with us when the storm starts to rage and things begin to look desperate. We can remember that we can speak to the storm, just as He did, and say, "Peace, be still." He has given us His authority to tread over all the power of the enemy (Luke 10:19).

As we draw near to Him, He draws near to us (James 4:8), and we can enjoy the full authority, power, and benefits of His presence.

From the Wilderness to the Land of Promise

Perhaps you are looking at your life and see that you've been in a place of perpetual dryness, desperation, and disillusionment. You have been crying out to God for deliverance. To you, the troubles in your life seem to look just like the Jordan River. You feel overtaken by them before you even step in. Their depth is too great, distance too wide, and current too fast. It looks as if there's no way to get over. It looks as if crossing over is impossible. But let me encourage you again—when you have the presence of God in your life, nothing is impossible. God will step in. He will make a way. He will open the way, He'll cause the river to stop, He'll part the river, and then you will cross over because you have the presence of God in your life. If He did it for the people of Israel then, He will make a way for you now, no matter what you are dealing with. God is the same yesterday, today, and forever.

Israel crossed over from the wilderness into the Promised Land and from the dry desert place into the fruitful land. Now God is taking you into the land flowing with milk and honey. You are coming out of your wilderness—your desperate place. You're coming out of your desert and your dry season. No more wilderness for your life!

I hear the Lord saying, "I'm bringing you to a land without scarceness. You will occupy a house you didn't build. You are going to drink from wells you didn't dig. You are going to eat from vineyards you didn't plant. You are going to dwell in a land flowing with milk and honey, a good land that the rain from heaven falls on."

> Then it shall be when the LORD your God brings you into the land which He swore to your fathers, to Abraham, Isaac, and Jacob, to give you great and fine cities, which you did not build, and houses full of all good things which you did not fill, and hewn cisterns which you did not dig, vineyards and olive trees which you did not plant, and you eat and are

> full, then beware lest you forget the LORD who brought you out of the land of Egypt, out of the house of bondage.
>
> —DEUTERONOMY 6:10–12

Get ready to cross over. Don't stay in the wilderness. Don't stay in the old. Cross over into the new. Go into the land that God has for you. Go into a new place. I know it's almost too good to believe, but I dare you to declare it aloud even now. Say, "I am crossing over into a good place."

Prayers for the Presence of God as You Cross Over

O Lord, let Your presence be upon my life. Let Your glory be in my life.

Do something new and fresh in my life, O God.

I believe that the presence of the Lord is in my life; His glory is in my life.

I will not cross over without the glory of God in my life.

I am going into a new place. It is being opened for me.

Lord, make a way for me to cross over into my inheritance and my blessing.

I will not go alone into this new land, but I'm going in with You. Your presence is with me.

By faith, I step into the water. I cross over into a new season of good things, in Jesus' name.

Lord, I receive the faith You are giving me to cross over.

Lord, I am ready to move into a new place. I am ready to cross over into a new place I've never lived in before and to inherit things I've never had before.

Lord, I am ready to possess things I never possessed before the loss.

Thank You, Lord, for bringing me over into a land full of prosperity and blessings. I will not lack.

Thank You, Lord, that I am not going in alone, but I'm going in with You. You go before me and open the way. Your presence is with me.

Lord, I receive Your command to step out in faith. I hear You say, "Don't stay where you are, but step out in faith."

I will not stay in the wilderness. By faith, I put my feet in the river and watch it roll back for me.

I declare that it is time for me to leave the dry place, the wilderness, the barren place, the place of temptation and testing, and to begin to move into a new land.

Lord, I'm believing You for good things. I hear You say, "I release good things into your life. No good thing will I withhold from them who walk uprightly."

It is my time to be released into a new realm of blessing, prosperity, favor, and grace. I declare that they will come upon me as I carry God's presence.

I will praise, worship, and dance before the Lord, and as I do I will see the way opened for me to cross over from death into life.

In the name of Jesus, I cross over from lack into more than enough, sickness into health and healing, curses into blessing, from where I am now into my destiny and future, and from old into new—new commissions, assignments, anointings, vision, dreams, songs, praise, worship, and even relationships.

In the name of Jesus, I break any spirits of doubt and unbelief. I believe the word of the Lord over my life. I will not die in the wilderness. I will cross over into a land flowing with milk and honey.

Chapter 5

A Thousand Times More

> May the LORD, the God of your fathers, make you one thousand times more numerous and bless you, just as He has promised you!
>
> —DEUTERONOMY 1:11

DEUTERONOMY IS A recording of God giving the Law again, this time to the generation who God declared would not be allowed to enter the Promised Land because of their unbelief. They would die in the wilderness, and their children, led by Joshua and Caleb, would be the ones to enter. At the beginning of Deuteronomy, Moses was reminding this dying generation of God's covenant, His Law. In it was their and their children's key to prosperity as they prepared to enter the land of Canaan. If they kept it, the blessing of the covenant would come upon them.[1]

In speaking this blessing, Moses used the word *thousand*: "May the LORD...make you one thousand times more numerous" (Deut. 1:11). As I read this, I began to meditate on the word *thousand*, because many times certain numbers have prophetic significance in the Bible. There are many references to *thousand* throughout the Scriptures. Here are some of the prophetic meanings God began to reveal to me about this number:

1. It is a symbol for perfection. One of the more popular references is Psalm 50:10, which says that "the cattle on one thousand hills" belong to Him. This is obviously not a literal thousand hills, as if the cattle on the one-thousand-first hill were not His. I then discovered that thousand is an all-inclusive number. It's a perfect number—ten times ten times ten.

2. It is a number that represents fullness. In the Book of Revelation, the redeemed reign with Christ for one thousand years. (See Revelation 20.) Some see these thousand years as a literal number, but really it is a number that represents complete perfection. It represents the redeemed fully entering into the kingdom.

3. It is a number of completion. Even the New Jerusalem, the Bible says, has the number *thousand* in it. In Revelation 21:14–21, its state of being complete and firmly built is represented by multiples of the number *one thousand*. There is also frequent mention of the number twelve, which represents government and the apostolic (v. 14). We see both these numbers appear in Revelation 21:16, where it says that the city measured twelve thousand furlongs.

4. It is a number that represents divine affection. The Bible says that God shows mercy to

a thousand generations. It doesn't mean there are only going to be a thousand generations. It's just a number that speaks of how long God's mercy will be extended to His people. God's mercy to us is part of His love and affection for us.

5. It is a number that speaks of miracles of increase and expansion. On the Day of Pentecost, there were several thousand who were saved (Acts 2:41). Jesus fed five thousand (Matt. 14:13–21), and then He also fed four thousand (Matt. 15:29–39).

6. It is a number that represents a heavenly level of worship. Daniel 7:10 tells us about the thousands upon thousands and ten thousand times ten thousand angels who ministered to the Lord. (This picture is also repeated in Revelation 5:11.) This means there were millions of angels worshipping the Lord, and the prophet used the number *thousands* to give us a picture of the height of worship in heaven.

7. It is a number that represents a level of giving that opens the heart of God. In 1 Kings 3:4–5 we see Solomon giving one thousand sacrifices when he dedicated the temple and God appearing to him asking, "Solomon, what do you want?" This is when Solomon asked Him for wisdom, and God gave him so much more.

God's Complete Blessing

The meaning that is central to what we are learning about how to break through desperate times is that *thousand* represents a realm of God's complete and full blessing on our lives. As God moved upon Moses's heart to repeat for His people His covenant to bless them as they prepared to cross over into the promise, He made it clear that this particular blessing was not regular. It was a blessing that would make them a thousand times more than what they were. They were a tiny nation. They were small, but God didn't choose them because they were many. Deuteronomy 7:7–9 says:

> The LORD did not set His love on you nor choose you because you were more in number than any of the peoples, for you were the fewest of all the peoples. But it is because the LORD loved you and because He kept the oath which He swore to your fathers. The LORD brought you out with a mighty hand and redeemed you out of the house of slavery, from the hand of Pharaoh, king of Egypt. Know therefore that the LORD your God, He is God, the faithful God, who keeps covenant and mercy with them who love Him and keep His commandments to a thousand generations.

If you read further into Deuteronomy 11, you will see that God's purpose for increasing them by the thousands was so they could be big enough to take the land, overcome the enemies that dwelled there, and possess all that He had for them. As they were increased, they would also possess more and more. They would never outgrow the fullness of God's blessing. His blessing, no matter how much they increased, would always be more than enough.

This is what I believe God wants to do in our lives as well. As we come out of the wilderness, the desert place, a season of testing, trial, and desperation, He wants to bless us and restore us, build us and refresh us a thousand times more so we can possess all that He has for us and still more. God wants you to cross over into a realm of fullness and completion, not partial blessings—a blessing here and a blessing there. We're not talking about blessings in answer to some of those prayers we sometimes pray: "Lord, just bless me any way You want to. Just give me a little dab, a little blessing." No. We're talking about a blessing that comes into your life and completely satisfies you.

Realize that we are among the evidence, the fruit, of God's thousands-more promise to Israel. Moses' prophetic pronouncement of this blessing includes us, the modern-day church; we are part of the increase of numbers that were to be added to Israel. Because of Christ we have been grafted into the seed of Abraham (Gal. 3:29). We have become the Israel of God. Along with the millions of believers in the world today, we are the fulfillment of God's promise to increase Israel by the thousands. In every nation, on every continent, and all across the globe, there are more believers on the planet today than at any other time in history. We are large enough to contain the full and complete blessing that God has for us in this hour, and we are still in line to receive the blessing of God that was pronounced all those thousands of years ago.

Understand also that this level of blessing is not something that comes from man. God is the one who pronounces the thousands-more type blessing upon every area in your life. And when He does it, there is nothing the devil, your family, your enemies, or anybody can do to stop it. Once it comes out by the anointing of God, it is settled in heaven. God will watch over His word to perform it. His blessings for us are so big that He must keep increasing the number of His people on the earth.

God wants to do more for us than we could ever imagine. We are the ones who limit God's blessings. We limit God. We get satisfied with so much. But I believe that whatever you are going through that led you to pick up this book and read it is also driving you to believe God for more. The season you are in is calling you higher. It's hard, I know. But it is also challenging you to ask, "Am I complete? Am I satisfied? Isn't there more to this thing than this?" It's challenging to remember who He has named you, that He has called you favor and has commanded His blessing toward you.

When God has released a word like this one in Deuteronomy 1:11, be confident that on the other side of the wilderness or desert His blessing is going to be so much bigger than you could ever imagine. A thousand times more. I mean, we'd get excited if it were doubled or tripled. We'd get excited about a hundredfold blessing. But a thousandfold? Listen, God is not the God of one, the God of two, the God of three, the God of four, the God of ten or even a hundred. He is the God of a thousand.

The Blessing of Giving in the Thousands Realm

> The king went to Gibeon to sacrifice there, for that was the great high place, and he offered one thousand burnt offerings on that altar. While he was in Gibeon, the LORD appeared to Solomon in a dream at night, and He said, "Ask what you want from Me."
>
> —1 KINGS 3:4–5

Throughout the course of my ministry, I have seen people give thousands, and through their giving, they have unlocked the blessings of the thousands realm. I want to be careful in making this next point. What I am about to discuss is not about giving more than what is in your heart to give or more than what you have. The Bible says that you should give according to the purposes in your heart, "not grudgingly or out of necessity, for God loves a cheerful giver" (2 Cor. 9:7). Some give fifty. Some one hundred. Give what you can. But how often have you heard that receiving is linked to giving? Luke 6:38 says, "Give, and it will be given to you: Good measure, pressed down, shaken together, and running over will men give unto you. For with the measure you use, it will be measured unto you." How often have you decreed and declared, "I'm blessed to be a blessing"?

I want to challenge you here, because the thousands realm is not only about your receiving a new level of blessing and increase. It is also about what is in your heart to give. A season may be coming in your life when you need to ask God to increase your heart in the area of giving and generosity. You may need to ask Him to increase the purposes of your heart so your giving will increase.

I've seen people enter the thousands realm in giving and receive access to God's blessings that surpassed what is usual. In 1 Kings 3 we learn the secret to how Solomon received his unusual anointing for wisdom and unmatched wealth. It's not always taught what happens before someone is promoted or a level of unusual blessing comes upon a person's life. We often just see the end result and want what they have, not realizing the cost. But in verse 4 it says that Solomon gave one thousand sacrifices. I could go into the amount of labor it took at that time to slaughter one thousand animals—the carnage, the blood, the stench, and the death. One thousand sacrifices, one thousand deaths. What had to die in order for Solomon to give and then receive in the thousands realm?

Of course, what we are reading here is about the old covenant way of giving an offering, but let's look at it prophetically, from the realm of the spirit. Their giving in the natural doesn't seem to compare to how some of us give. When we are presented with an opportunity to give to the Lord, some of us look in our purses or wallets; pull out a checkbook, card, or cash; drop a little something in the offering plate or bucket; and move on without much thought or effort. There is no physical or spiritual exertion, no bloodshed, no hardship or sacrifice. Now, don't mistake what I am saying. Christ died, and our debt has been paid. This is not about the sin offering or atonement. This is about the spirit and intention behind our giving to God. Maybe there is a realm we need to go to in our giving where we are more purposeful and challenged to give more in order to receive an unusual level of blessing and breakthrough.

After Solomon gave one thousand sacrifices, verse 5 says that God showed up and told him, "Ask what you want from Me." Does your giving cause God to show up to you personally, one-on-one, and say, "Ask Me for whatever you want"? Can you imagine? What would you ask for? A Cadillac or some other material thing? Would you leave it open for Him to decide—"However You want to bless me, God, bless me"? Well, Solomon was specific, and he didn't ask for anything material and temporary. He asked for wisdom.

If we're honest, most of us would have never asked for wisdom, but that was the smartest thing to ask for. You know why? Wisdom brings all the blessings of God. When you have wisdom, you have everything you need.

But Solomon wasn't given this rare opportunity with God until after he offered God one thousand sacrifices. As I studied this, I wondered, what made him not just give one sacrifice or two or even three? He gave one thousand because there is something significant about that number. Some of us need to increase our giving into that thousands realm. We like to receive in the thousands realm, but thinking about giving in that realm starts to feel a little uncomfortable.

As we pray to enter the realm where we receive thousands-level blessings, we need to also pray about coming into another realm of giving. We need to break out of this realm of just having enough. We need to begin to think in terms of thousands. We need to begin to think bigger. God is so big. He is a God of thousands.

Something Big, Something Fast

> A little one shall become a thousand, and a small one a strong nation. I, the Lord, will hasten it in its time.
>
> —Isaiah 60:22

God's blessing is represented by a thousand. In looking at Isaiah 60:22, I believe that a thousand is a symbol of something big. I believe that God is saying there is a time when He will command His blessing, and He is going to do it quickly. There are a couple of scriptures that I like concerning this. One is Deuteronomy 28:8:

> The Lord will command the blessing on you in your barns and in all that you set your hand to do, and He will bless you in the land which the Lord your God is giving you.

And the other one is Amos 9:13 (The Message):

> "Yes indeed, it won't be long now." God's Decree.
>
> "Things are going to happen so fast your head will swim, one thing fast on the heels of the other. You won't be able to keep up. Everything will be happening at once—and everywhere you look, blessings! Blessings like wine pouring off the mountains and hills."

God is going to make His blessing come upon you quickly. The blessing will not take a long time to manifest. He is going to take you—a little one—and make you a thousand. He is going to multiply you by a thousand.

The number *one thousand* is symbolic, and the verse in

Isaiah 60 is about a prophetic blessing. We've already discussed what the number *one thousand* represents. In many ways it is a picture of living in the kingdom. When you come into the kingdom, you step into a realm that is supernatural. When you come into the kingdom, you step into a realm of multiplication. When you come into the kingdom, you step into the realm where limits are broken. When you come into the kingdom, you can come in poor, depressed, discouraged, and cursed, but you also step into the blessing of God. When you are in the kingdom and you get around the prophetic word of God, the presence of God, and the King of kings, and He releases His scepter upon your life, He can do more in you in a quick period of time than man can do in a lifetime.

God said, "I am going to do something so quick and so big in your life. I am going to command a thousandfold blessing upon your life. I am going multiply you and put a call, an anointing, a purpose, a blessing, or a mantle on you that man cannot put on you. I am going to bring you into the eternal realm, the realm of the spirit and of thousands. I am going to bring you into the millennium realm."

This is not just an earthly thing we've been talking about in this chapter. We are talking about an eternity of blessing and increase. We are talking about the new heaven and new earth, one thousand years of lions and wolves living together (Isa. 11:6). God is thinking about His kingdom and bringing us into His perfection and completion. He is bringing us into a place of the impossible where the miraculous is an everyday occurrence, the place where people may say it cannot happen, but God will supernaturally command it to be so. People may have cursed you and said, "You will never have anything. You will never produce. You will never be anything." They may have questioned your faith. But God is a rewarder of those who diligently seek Him (Heb. 11:6), and He is saying now, "I am commanding My blessing to be released to you."

What God is planning for you will astound your adversaries and confuse your enemies. They will ask, "How in the world did you get what you have?" And you will tell them, "It's not by might. It's not by power, but it's by the Spirit of the Lord (Zech. 4:6). God has commanded His blessing upon my life!"

Prayers That Release the Thousands-More Blessing

Thank You, Lord, that by faith I can step into the thousands realm, God's realm, the realm of the unlimited, the realm of the spirit, the realm of the blessing of God.

I step out of the old into the new, into a new place of giving and receiving.

Let a multiplication anointing come upon my life.

Whatever has to die in my life to position me to receive this anointing, let it die, Lord.

Something great is about to happen in my life. Something new is about to happen. I will not settle for anything less. I confess a thousandfold blessing to come upon my life.

Lord, bless my finances by a thousand. Bless my church by a thousand. Bless my ministry by a thousand. Let a multiplication anointing come upon my life.

Lord, make the little one a thousand.

Lord, You do unusual things. I pray that You will do the unusual in my life.

God, I pray that You will bless me and multiply me. Release Your grace, favor, peace, and prosperity upon my life.

Lord, bring me into the thousands realm. Let thousands upon thousands upon thousands come upon me in the name of Jesus.

Lord, as I give, increase my capacity to give into the thousands realm. As I give a thousandfold, let me receive the thousandfold blessing upon my life in the name of Jesus. Bless me so that I may be a blessing.

I decree and prophesy that I am about to enter into another realm of blessing, an unlimited realm of unlimited favor and finances in the name of Jesus.

Chapter 6

God's Glory Released

> May his name endure forever; may his name increase as long as the sun. May men be blessed in him; may all nations call him blessed! Blessed be the LORD God, the God of Israel, who alone does wondrous deeds. Blessed be His glorious name forever; and may the whole earth be filled with His glory. Amen, and Amen. The prayers of David the son of Jesse are ended.
>
> —PSALM 72:17–20

IN THE PREVIOUS chapters we saw how Hannah persevered through her season of barrenness and unfruitfulness and went from beseeching God with persistent and desperate prayers to prophesying once again. Her focus moved from her situation (when she was in need) to the condition of her nation as the Lord revealed the greater purpose for the promise that was birthed through her. Though her desperate times had been relieved, her nation was also facing a desperate time, since there had not been a prophetic word released to them for some time.

Because she had been delivered, she had faith to stand in the gap for her people: "The LORD makes poor and makes rich," she prophesied. "He brings low and lifts up. He raises up the poor out of the dust and lifts up the oppressed from the dunghill to make them sit with princes and inherit a throne of glory" (1 Sam. 2:7–8). She was prophesying the blessing of the Lord, that her people would soon inherit a throne of glory.

As you cross over from desperation to fulfillment, realize that what you have received from God is not just for you. Your time being perfected in the wilderness—the strength, faith, and boldness you received during that time—has prepared you to believe for that same level of increase, blessing, deliverance, and prosperity to be released in the earth.

It is time to pray desperate prayers for more than just you and yours. You need to begin to pray desperate prayers for the desperate times in our world. God wants all the nations of the earth to know His power, love, and favor. As Hannah began to speak out God's will for her nation, God is calling you to speak out of what He has done for you and to proclaim His glory in the earth.

Aligning With God's Plan for the Earth

No matter where you go in the world—what language people speak, what color they are, or what their culture is—every person has within them a desire to connect with God, to come into contact with the living God and experience His presence. Many don't understand what that yearning is, but they are seeking God's glory. God has placed something inside of us, every one of us, that really yearns to come into contact with heaven, to know the power, atmosphere, anointing, and glory of heaven. And so God has made a way through the gospel, the church, preaching, and teaching that His glory can be experienced throughout the entire world, and the earth will be full of His glory.

What I love about the particular passage in the Psalm that started this chapter is that it gives us, I believe, God's plan for the earth. It is found in verse 19: "Blessed be His glorious name forever; and may the whole earth be filled with His glory."

It has always been the will of God for the entire earth to be filled with His glory, for every nation, kindred, and tongue to experience His presence, favor, and power. My ministry teams and I are witnessing an expansion of God's glory happening as we minister around the world. We're seeing great churches full of God's glory being raised up in different parts of the world. We're seeing people of all languages and cultures come into contact with the presence of God through worship, praise, hearing the Word of God, and God's manifest glory.

This has always been God's plan. When He spoke to Abraham and said, "In you all the families (nations) of the earth will be blessed" (Gen. 12:3, AMP), it was never only about Israel. It was always about the entire world. God used Israel as a covenant people through whom the Messiah would come, and from their land—Jerusalem—the gospel would go out into all the world. This is why Jesus gave the command to preach the gospel to every creature.

Before any of this came to pass, David saw, by the Spirit of God, the entire world being full of the glory of God. And it could have only been revealed to Him by God, because David had lived his entire life within Israel's small territory and had never gone outside of it, except when he was running from Saul and went into the land of the Philistines. In other words, his prayer life and his prophetic mantle took him outside of the place he lived and showed him the full purpose and plan of God, not only for his entire nation but also for the entire earth. His vision was not limited. He was not limited by where he lived and by what he saw in the natural. He had a vision to go outside of that to see the entire world full of the glory of God.

A Vision for the Nations

I believe that if you're going to have a kingdom mentality, you must have a mentality that the desires, dreams, and visions God gives you are not just for your city, family, or church but for the entire world. God is much bigger than your church. He's much bigger than your denomination. The problem that churches often have is that their vision gets limited to their church or denomination. They don't look outside of that. They don't have a world vision.

But God wants us to have a vision for the nations. He says, "Ask of Me, and I will give you the nations for your inheritance, and the ends of the earth for your possession" (Ps. 2:8). We often talk about possessing the land and being blessed and delivered, healed and set free from a personal perspective. But the blessing of the Lord is also for the world to see that God is real, and His presence and glory are available for all.

When you come into contact with the prophetic anointing and the Spirit of God gets in your life, you'll begin to see outside of your family, the four walls of your church, and your city limits. You'll begin to have a vision that is far greater than what you can see in the natural, because the Spirit of God will begin to show you the plan of God, which is much greater than you and your family, church, and denomination.

We need the Spirit of God to help us see beyond what we see in the natural and our circumstances or surroundings. If you were ever to meet anyone from my church or in my ministry, they would all tell you I encourage people to travel because when you go to different places and see different things, you are able break ignorance out of your life and expand your worldview. If you can't travel, get a book and read about somewhere else. The world is much larger than you realize.

More than 7.5 billion people live on this planet, and whether they know it or not, they want to come into contact with the glory of God. When you begin to allow the Spirit of God to speak to your heart beyond your own life situations, you will begin to pray prayers that will stir your vision for the world.

Beyond Your Understanding

When the glory of God comes into your life and you've been filled afresh with His Spirit, I believe that God will begin to speak things to you that you have never thought of before. I believe that you are going to pray in ways you never thought you would pray before. The Spirit of God will lead you beyond your understanding of the way you see the world and even yourself.

David is an example of this. He was a Jew living in Israel. He was limited to that nation and did not go outside of that nation. All he could see with his natural eyes was Israel and its twelve tribes, and the temple in Jerusalem. But in the spirit, in prayer, God took him beyond his land to the point where he prayed, "Let the earth—the entire world—be full of the glory of God." (See Psalm 72:19.) In other words, God wanted him to see beyond his own area and era to a time when the entire planet would experience His glory.

That's what the prophetic anointing does. That's what happens when you pray prophetically. God will take your beginning prayer and your interpretation and by His Spirit begin to pray through you things that are beyond your natural understanding. You will begin to pray things that people will say are crazy. The Spirit of God will break the limitations off your mind. This is why I often teach that the prophetic is more than just speaking forth the word of the Lord. The prophetic includes your prayer life. It includes your worship life. It includes the songs you sing and the divine utterances that come out of your mouth. It includes having a prophetic mentality through which God takes your prayers to places in the spirit that you've never been before.

Traveling in the spirit

While in Africa for a ministry trip, one of the ministers who traveled with me told me years ago he'd had a vision of coming to the place at which we had just arrived. He said he saw the street and the people whom we were ministering to. He said God had taken him in the spirit and showed him the place we were in.

I believe God can take you places in the spirit even before you physically get there. I know that's deep for some people, and this may be a problem with the church. We talk about the Holy Spirit and say we believe in His power, but we don't expect to walk fully in that power. So when we hear about supernatural things like what I just described, people think the testimony is flaky, weird, and just too spiritual and deep. But that's the Spirit of God; He can do anything. The Spirit of God isn't limited by our natural circumstances, and He has a concern for the entire planet, for the entire world.

God can take you out of that place of limitation and bring you to places you've never dreamed you could go. This is what makes serving God an adventure. It should always be exciting to serve God. It should never be boring or routine. Serving Him should not only be about going to church and having a nice, religious service. Who wants to serve a boring God? Who wants to live a boring, average life with no miracles, breakthroughs, or glory? Who wants to live a life with God where there is nothing new and fresh, nothing miraculous and supernatural? We all want to experience the glory and supernatural power of God that comes through the Holy Ghost.

Answering the Macedonian Call

Here is my testimony of how God took me beyond everything I had known and gave me a desire to see the nations filled with His glory. I grew up in the hood on the South Side of Chicago. For most of my younger years I never went anywhere, and I had never been on a plane. I went to camp once. It was the Salvation Army camp, and I only went because it was free. My family didn't own a car, but I thank

God that they loved me and took care of me. However, since I came into contact with the Holy Spirit and the power of God, God has taken me to places I didn't even know were on a map. Those opportunities were not by might, nor by power, but by the Spirit of God.

I often tell this story of my first trip to the Solomon Islands. As our plane approached the island, it was immediately rerouted. We couldn't fly in directly. We had to go through Australia to a city called Honiara in the Solomon Islands. Once we landed, I found out that they were in a civil war, which is something you should tell the guest speaker before he comes. In finding this out, my thought was, "Please, let me preach, and get me out of there." I didn't know what they were fighting about, but I didn't have anything to do with it. They tried to reassure me by telling me, "It's OK. The rebels are outside the city." I was thinking, "They are outside the city? But when are they arriving? I want to know when they are getting here."

That morning they found three heads cut off in baskets in the marketplace. I told the Lord, "God, this is really going well. Civil war. Heads cut off. And I have to preach. What do You want me to tell these people?" Finally, He gave me a word, and I got up and preached to about eight hundred people, many of them young people. It was an outdoor meeting. I preached a message that was fresh on my heart at the time; it was about when God gives you a message about going to the nations. I asked, "How many want to go?" Everyone ran up to the altar. They were trying to get off that island. They were ready for a word. They would have gone anywhere but where they were.

At the end of the service, they begged us to pray for them.

As we did, the power of God hit that place, and those young people began to fall out. We prophesied to them. It was amazing. It was one of the most anointed services I had ever seen, and it was in a place I had never been—a place in the middle of a civil war where people's heads were being cut off. It was a mess in the natural, but the word of the Lord came and His power fell because God loves people. It was amazing what happened there.

While I was thanking God that I could get on a plane and get out of there, I couldn't help but also think about my being a person from the South Side of Chicago preaching the power of God in the Solomon Islands. I had never even heard of that place. I had never been there before. I hadn't really been anywhere at that point. But there I was on a remote island in the Pacific, prophesying and laying hands on all these leaders. That is how God's glory fills the earth. It starts with a fire in us, and we take it to the ends of the earth.

Sometime later we took a team to a nation called Vanuatu, another island in the South Pacific. Have you ever heard of it? A season of the TV show *Survivor* was filmed there. Even though I obviously wasn't on the show, I feel like I can say I survived Vanuatu. It is full of jungles, and it is so hot and humid that my team members were fainting. But we prayed, preached, and ministered to the people there, a people who for many years I didn't even know existed.

God is able to take you places you never imagined you would go, because there is always a Macedonian call. (See Acts 16:6–10.) There's always someone saying, "Come over and help us." There's always someone saying, "We need the word of the Lord. We need deliverance. We need teaching."

God will cause you to be assigned to go to places you never imagined.

Going to the nations is not necessarily for everyone. Your assignment may be in your own city or somewhere in the United States. But I want to give you what I believe is a prophetic understanding of how God causes men like David to pray prophetically for the entire world to be full of the glory of God. As I have said, it has always been God's plan for the earth to experience His glory, presence, power, and Spirit. It has always been His plan for people of all nations to come into contact with His glory with true worship. In this atmosphere, God speaks to us, we get healed, we get delivered and blessed, and we encounter the power and presence of God, which changes our lives forever.

Not Only for Heaven

The glory of God is not for heaven only. It's for the earth as well. God wants you to experience His glory while you are living on this planet. No person should live without the glory of God in his life. Every one of us can experience God's glory and His presence. In fact, God created you to experience His glory. If you're not experiencing His glory, you're living beneath your privilege as a child of God. If you're not experiencing the presence and the glory and the anointing of God, you're living below your privilege as a human being.

Before you got here, people prayed for you. David was one of these people. He prayed generations ago that you would experience God's glory. But David was one among many throughout the generations praying that God would show you His glory. In other words, you are here and you have an opportunity to experience God's glory not only because of what you are praying now but because somebody prayed before you got here.

Thank God somebody prayed for the glory of God to touch this generation. Thank God somebody prayed for Chicago, for America, for the earth, and for the nations to experience the glory of God. That person may be dead now—you may meet him in heaven one day—but thank God someone prayed so that you and I could encounter God, so that we could be saved, so that we could experience what we are experiencing today. Thank God someone who did not even know us prayed before we got here: "Lord, visit the earth. Lord, release Your glory. Lord, send revival. Lord, raise up Your people. Lord, manifest Your power." And so here we are experiencing the glory of God in our generation.

But guess what? God doesn't just want us to experience His glory. God wants us to pray that the coming generations will also experience what we are experiencing here. God wants us to pray for God to show up in nations where there is no glory and begin to raise up His church in those places. Let me put it this way: Someone prayed for you. You were delivered. Your prayers were answered. Your needs were met. You've crossed over into shalom, the full peace and blessing of the Lord. Now it's time for you to pray for someone else. It's time for you to stand in the house of God and lift your hands and say, "God, show Your glory. Touch the next generation. Move in America. Manifest Your power. Let someone who is not yet born encounter You, O God, when he comes into this earth. Let him live for You."

Your Prayers Don't End Until His Glory Comes

Listen to this: your prayers do not end until you pray for the glory of God to touch the earth. Your prayers do not come to an end until you ask God to fill the earth with His glory. That's when David's prayers came to an end, when he asked God to move beyond himself, his people, and his nation.

This is not about my glory or yours; it's about His glory. This is not about me or you, my church, your church, how big our ministries are, or how great we are. It's not about my title or your title and what people call us. It's not about how many members I have, how many television stations I'm on, or how many books I've written. It's not about me and my ministry, my calling, and my anointing. It's only about one thing, and that is the glory of God. Let Him be glorified. It's not about us; it's about Him.

Only One Thing Is Eternal

Once we get our minds off ourselves and realize that we are created for His glory, He'll bless, promote, and exalt us. He made David king. I mean, I'm amazed at David. He was a shepherd boy who was on the back side of the desert keeping sheep. He wasn't even important enough for Jesse, his father, to call him when Samuel came to anoint the next king of Israel. (See 1 Samuel 16.) But Samuel stood before each one of David's brothers and said, "He's not the one," until there was no one left. When he turned to Jesse and asked if he had any other sons, he said, "Yes. I have a little boy named David." As soon as David walked in, God said, "He's the one. I poured the anointing on him."

God will take you from being a nobody to being a somebody when He sees that you will promote His will in the earth. This is why we get delivered and set free: so that there is no hindrance between God and us, and He is able to pour His glory in us and through us. God is able to exalt you.

What I love about David is that regardless of how God promoted him, he understood that one day he would die. He understood that one day he would not be living on the earth. He understood that one day he would die and go to be with God. He understood that everything he saw was temporary and limited. There's only one thing that is eternal, and it's the glory of God.

As a believer who understands that you have a number of years on this earth, that you are not going to live forever, your prayer focus should be, "Lord, I know beyond my life there is something so important. It's called your glory. Lord, I know there are people who have not yet experienced what I've experienced, and I cannot rest as long as I know there are lost people living in darkness who've never experienced what I have."

Of course, while you're living on this planet, you can enjoy life and family and friends. You can enjoy the things God has given you. It's good to go to church and praise and worship, encounter God, and be blessed and touched by His glory. But when all of that is over, there's still somebody who needs to be saved. There's still somebody who doesn't know the glory of God.

Let your prayer be, "Lord, let Your glory touch my family. Let Your glory touch my neighborhood. Let Your glory touch my city. But beyond that, Lord, let it touch Africa, Europe, and Asia. Let it touch South America. Let it touch the islands of the sea. Lord, let Your glory touch all flesh."

When you begin to pray beyond yourself and you get God's vision for the whole earth, you will not be able to keep it to yourself. Hannah didn't. David didn't. When you touch God, you will not be able to keep your mouth shut.

God's Glory Changes Your Prayers

As you cross over into a place of shalom—blessing, peace, and prosperity—into your promised land, where the covenant blessings of God have been released to you, you will begin to imagine how life would be if everyone had access to this same level of blessing. This is what the glory of God will do in your life. It will change how you pray and how you think about the world around you. Once you come into contact with God's glory, you will pray like David prayed: "To see Your power and Your glory, as I've seen You in the sanctuary. Oh, to see Your glory fill the earth!" (Ps. 63:2, author's paraphrase).

This is the prayer of someone who has encountered the glory of God, whose life God has touched. No wonder David was praying for the earth to be filled with the glory of God. Once you experience God's presence and glory, you cannot keep it a secret. You want to share it with everybody you come into contact with. Once you come into contact with the glory, power, and grace of God, you tell your family, friends, enemies, and even other nations.

Because somebody prayed, "Let Your glory fill the earth," a day is coming when those who don't know God will call on His name and be saved. People sometimes look at North Africa—Algeria, Mali, Libya, Egypt, and other predominantly Muslim nations—with little expectation of the glory of God being able to penetrate their regions. But God says, "I'm able to change them too. My glory is coming to Egypt. It's coming to Libya, Algeria, and Morocco. My glory will fill the earth." It may not happen in my lifetime, but a day is coming when Muslim nations will call on the name of Jesus. A day is coming when people will stop watching the bad news and start praying for revival. A day is coming when people will stop looking at how messed up the world is and see beyond what things look like in the natural—beyond the trouble, war, and pain—and see the glory.

It takes prophetic people to see the glory. Prophetic people can step into a mess and say, "I see glory coming out of this." A prophet can come into a person's life when it is all messed up and say, "I see beyond this. I see God bringing you out. I see God restoring you. I see miracles. I see healing. I see power. I see glory." We need people who can see beyond. We need people who can step into a nation and begin to prophesy that revival is coming. We need people who will get on their knees and pray prophetically for the glory of God to be released. Are you one of these people?

Pray Beyond

I challenge you to begin to pray beyond your circumstances, beyond your life, and even beyond your lifetime, your generation. Your prayers do not have to be limited to now. You can pray twenty or thirty years into the future. This is another case for why we as Spirit-filled believers ought to pray in tongues. The Holy Ghost can take your tongues and help you pray beyond and into a time you won't even be here in the earth. But your prayers will still be here.

David has been dead for thousands of years, but his prayer lives today. His prayer is being fulfilled today. The glory of God is touching the earth today. I imagine David prayed a prayer something like this:

> *God, let the earth be full of Your glory. Let every nation experience Your glory. Let every color, tribe, and tongue worship You. Let them bow down and come into contact with Your glory. Lord, You are bigger than my nation. You are bigger than my family. You are bigger than my throne. You are bigger than anything I'm able to do. You're able to do exceedingly abundantly. Let my prayer go beyond what I am able to see in the natural. Let every nation of the earth in every time from here to eternity be filled with Your glory.*

That is why I love the prophetic. The prophetic makes you bigger than you are. The prophetic makes your prayers go deeper and farther than you could ever go in the natural. When you're prophetic, your words release things that go beyond what you can see. Your words carry an anointing, and they're able to take you places that you could not go before. As you pray, believe for glory to be released more than just this month and this year. When you pray, believe that God will prophetically expand the territory and time of your prayers, that they will go beyond what you can see in the natural and that people in this age and the next who have never encountered God's glory will. Believe that something supernatural is going to happen because of your glory prayers.

Prayers to Release God's Glory

Lord, let the entire earth—people I've never met, strangers I've never known, places I've never been, places I'll never go—experience your glory.

Let the next generation of sons and daughters be raised up, Lord. Raise up preachers, prophets, apostles, evangelists, pastors, teachers, minstrels, psalmists, churches and houses of glory, and worshippers so the earth comes into contact with Your glory and power.

Let miracles, signs and wonders, healing, deliverance, and other manifestations of Your glory arise.

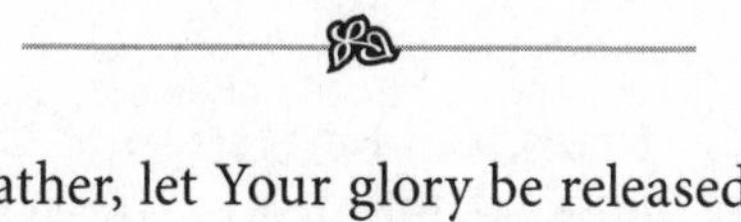

Father, let Your glory be released.

Let the earth be full of Your glory. Let my nation, city, and church be full of Your glory. Let my family encounter Your glory.

Lord, I am here for Your glory—not my glory or any man's glory, but only Your glory, God.

Lord, let me not only see miracles, signs and wonders, healings, deliverances, salvations, and breakthroughs. Let me walk in the power of Your glory.

Lord, I pray now for a release of Your power and anointing.

Lord, I pray for this generation and generations to come, that we all will experience Your glory.

Lord, I thank You for seasons of testing, trial, and hardship that purify me and prove me to be a worthy glory carrier.

Lord, I am a willing vessel. Let me carry Your glory to the ends of the earth. Let Your glory be evident in every area of my life.

Chapter 7

When the Glory Comes

> The earth belongs to the LORD, and its fullness, the world, and those who dwell in it.
>
> —PSALM 24:1

GOD OWNS THE earth, and everything in it belongs to Him. When He releases the fullness of His glory into the earth, we have a responsibility to steward it. We know from the mandate God gave man in Genesis 1:26–28 that He has given us dominion and authority over the earth. He said:

> Let Us make man in Our image, after Our likeness, and let them have dominion over the fish of the sea, and over the birds of the air, and over the livestock, and over all the earth, and over every creeping thing that creeps on the earth.…Be fruitful and multiply, and replenish the earth and subdue it. Rule over the fish of the sea and over the birds of the air and over every living thing that moves on the earth.

We lost this authority at the fall of Adam and Eve, through which humankind entered into sin. But then God returned it to us through the death and resurrection of His Son, Jesus, often referred to as the second or last Adam. In the Gospel of Matthew Jesus taught that "all authority has been given to Me in heaven and on earth" (28:18) and that He would authorize us to use His authority to bind and loose things on earth as they are in heaven (16:19). And in Luke 10:19 we learn that He gave us "authority to trample on serpents and scorpions, and over all the power of the enemy."

Even as God releases His glory and redemption into the earth, we have a part to play in the condition of the planet and how it is maintained physically, spiritually, politically, and otherwise. Often people will say that everything that happens on earth is the will of God, but that's not entirely true. It is not the will of God for people to die in sin. It's their choice. It is not the will of God for terrible things to happen. God desires for the planet to be blessed. He did not create it to be cursed, and though it was cursed through our actions and choices, He has done all He could to return the dominion of the earth to us. So much of what happens on earth has a lot to do with the authority we exercise.

The Hebrew word for *earth* in Psalm 24:1 means "land."[1] So it's as if God is saying the condition of the land that you live on—wherever you live; the city, region, nation, or territory—depends on what decisions the people who live on that land have made. It depends on the government, the way the people live, the decisions they make, how and what they worship, and what is taught. The condition of the land—whether it is blessed or cursed—will depend on the decisions we make as the inhabitants of the land, and this includes how God's glory is able to infiltrate the area and make a lasting impact.

Choose Life

> I call heaven and earth to witnesses against you this day, that I have set before you life and death, blessing and curse. Therefore choose life, that both you and your descendants may live.
>
> —DEUTERONOMY 30:19

People blame God or the devil for many things that are the result of their own choices—the things they choose to do, the decisions they choose to make, and the condition they find themselves in. I know we've been talking about desperate times as a means of testing, but it is important for us to do some soul-searching in these times, especially when it seems that the testing or desperate situation we are facing is beyond us and more connected to the environment we find ourselves in.

Sometimes economic, social, religious, or political unrest are at the root of some of the desperate times we face. Sometimes the condition we are in is a result of the decisions we've made because of the environment we've come up in. But this does not absolve us of our responsibility as believers to be delivered so we can rise above these circumstances and begin to use our authority and power to make choices that lead to life as we come into God's wisdom, knowledge, and understanding.

Often we don't want to take responsibility, so when situations in our lives or on the planet are out of control, we say things like, "Where is God? Why doesn't God change this? Why doesn't God intervene in this?" But we are missing the powerful role that we play and the effects of our collective decisions.

Injustice and many of the things that seem to be so far out of order are a result of our decisions. The wrong people are in authority. The wicked are in control. The righteous are suffering. This is not the plan of God. So anytime you see situations like this, your response cannot be, "God, where are You?" While the world is doing as it chooses, we as believers have a choice too. We can take responsibility and choose the actions that lead to life. We can stand up in our God-given authority and say, "If God has given me the responsibility of the earth, that means I have authority here, and that means I can do something about the situation. I am not a victim. I am not helpless. I don't just sit back and let things happen. I have authority on the planet, and I choose life."

We can change things. We can rectify things. We can do something about the situation. We don't have to sit by and allow things to get out of control, feeling like helpless victims, believing for the rapture and eternal escape. We can pray.

Governing the Earth Through Prayer

As I pointed out in an earlier chapter, God will intervene. He will send deliverance and His glory in answer to our prayers. Prayer is part of how we exercise the authority He has given us to bind and loose things in the earth. When we pray, we literally invite God to come into a situation. When we pray, we pray recognizing that we are stewards and cannot turn things around on our own. We pray expressing our dependence on God's grace, mercy, wisdom, and power. Then God in His mercy responds to our prayers and begins to correct, rectify, and change things, and put them back in order.

We pray and we prophesy because we know if things are not right, we can ask for God's intervention. We know that the word of the Lord coming out of our mouths will cause God to intervene and cause change to come. Psalm 24:1 is really telling us about the tremendous amount of authority we have as believers to assist God in governing the earth through our prayers.

Sometimes we find ourselves facing such desperate times on our planet. The things we see in our nations and cities and on the news are astounding, heartbreaking, overwhelming, and sad. The devil wants to make us feel as if we are insignificant and helpless. He tries to make us feel as if it won't make any difference whether we pray or prophesy, because things look so bad. But those of us who have faith know that if we believe God, we can see change. From family and financial crises to the crime and corruption in our cities, it may look like everything is going crazy. Wherever the trouble is, as saints of God we should be quick to understand that if God has given us authority on this planet, then we can stand up and do something. We can pray because God has given us the authority in the earth to pray and come before Him and see Him act on our behalf.

Don't Draw Back

Psalm 24:1 is very important because it really puts the responsibility of the planet in our hands. Sometimes the reason things have gone bad is because the people of God have withdrawn. The church doesn't get involved. The church is preaching about the rapture and escape. We are preaching messages that everything is getting worse, which leaves many feeling as if their prayers won't matter anyway.

My thinking is this: Does it have to get worse? If it is going to get worse, what's the use of praying? If God is not going to intervene, why pray? It's almost as if there is no point in believing for revival, looking for God's glory to fill the earth, or expecting anything to change. Or can we pray and change some things?

Imagine if before the Civil War, people who were opposed to slavery had said, "It's just going to get worse anyway," and gave up. Slavery would never have been abolished, and many of our lives would not look the way they do today. If they had drawn back and had no hope for a better future, that change would never have happened.

Listen, you cannot just resign your life, your family, your city, your nation, or this planet to the devil. We need some people who know how to stand up and say, "Devil, you are a liar. You will not take this land."

But often we don't have any faith for that. We can believe God for our healing or maybe financial breakthrough, but when it comes to the people of God believing Him for transformation on a local and global scale, our faith level is low. We don't really believe our cities and nations can be changed.

Wrong Teaching Can Hurt Our Faith

Some end-times teaching about everything getting worse has stripped the church of its power and authority. We come to church, sing songs, and listen to a sermon, all while believing everything is going to get worse, but one day soon we will escape it, and the Lord is going to come and take us home. This line of teaching—and I hear it a lot in churches—sometimes causes us to just let the devil have his way. What we hear is often what we put faith in, because faith comes by hearing (Rom. 10:17). However, you can believe and have faith that your prayers are effective even during the last days.

We need to question our line of thinking here: Where is the dominion of the church when things look dire? Where is our power? Where are our authority and faith? Who are we? Are we just a bunch of people trying to get to heaven? Are we just a bunch of people stuck in the last days? Are we just a bunch of people who have to accept that everything is getting worse, that our desperate situations are irreversible signs of the times? Are we supposed to just watch our cities and nations be destroyed by perversion and witchcraft and believe we can't do anything about it? No! The Bible says ask and you will receive. Seek and you will find. Knock and the door will be opened (Matt. 7:7). You can make a difference.

The devil uses any means he can, including certain teachings, to make you feel as if you are helpless, that you are just one person whose prayers aren't working. He wants to make you think God isn't hearing your prayers and you are fighting a losing battle.

The truth is, sometimes problems do make you want to just run and hide. They tempt you to say, "Just let me close my door. I'm going to mind my own business because it's too crazy out there." Sometimes you want to say, "God, this is Your planet. It's Yours, Lord. I give it back to You. I know

You gave it to me, but You can have it back. I never asked for it, Lord. I just came here and grew up. This is a mess."

But God says, "No. I gave you the authority on the planet, and so whenever things are not right, it's your responsibility to turn them around." This is why God said, "If My people, who are called by My name, will humble themselves and pray, and seek My face and turn from their wicked ways, then I will hear from heaven, and will forgive their sin and will heal their land" (2 Chron. 7:14).

What God is saying here is, "My people have to do something if they want the land to be healed. It's not up to Me. Things do not have to stay the way they are. They can get better. They can turn around." It is not up to Him. He has already stated what He wants. He wants His glory to fill the earth. What do we want? If we want what He wants, will we pray? Will we humble ourselves? Will we turn from our wicked ways?

Prayer, humility, and repentance are keys to being able to sustain a release of God's glory. They are keys to seeing a manifestation of God's power in the earth. God hears the prayers of the righteous and the humble. He is quick to answer their prayers because they pray in line with His perfect will. Releasing His glory and bringing deliverance and healing to the land is His perfect will for the earth. He has given His people the authority to activate His power through prayer, but we must come boldly to the throne of grace. We cannot run away from our responsibility. We must have faith that our prayers make a difference and bring transformation to the most desperate situations.

Don't Go by How It Looks

Even when it seems like things are only getting worse—and I know you've been there—remember that we walk by faith and not by sight (2 Cor. 5:7). When you go by how the situation looks, you'll always be depressed. But when you see with the eyes of faith, you'll say to any mountain in front of you, "Be removed and be thrown into the sea" (Mark 11:23), and you will not doubt that it will happen. You will believe that what you say will come to pass. You can have what you say when you have faith. Nothing is impossible to him who believes (Mark 9:23). Nothing.

Faith changes things. "Faith is the substance of things hoped for, the evidence of things not seen" (Heb. 11:1). Even though you don't see what you are believing for, you have it because you have faith. You can't go by how the situation looks because it can change any day. God has given you faith to change things.

If you want to see some things changed in your life, your family, or your church, I dare you to declare right now that whatever needs to change and line up with the word of the Lord over your life can't remain the same. Say, "It has to change because I'm here. When I open my mouth, something is going to change. When I decree, something is going to change. When I prophesy, something is going to change. When I say new things, something is going to change. My finances are going to change. My family is going to change. My situation is going to change. Because greater is He who is in me than he who is in the world."

What Are You Going to Do With What God Gave You?

God has given us authority down here on earth. God says, "I gave you the planet." What are we going do with it? He gave it to Adam, but he lost it. Are you going to follow his pattern? Are you going to let the devil lie to you and keep you from praying? Are you going to sit back and let him run over you and your family? Or are you going to stand up and say, "Enough is enough"? Are you going to be bold enough to say, "Whatever I bind on earth is bound in heaven. Whatever I loose on earth is loosed in heaven"? What are you going to do with what He has given you?

I often pray for the city where I live and pastor. There are lots of areas in Chicago that need prayer desperately. Whenever I go around the world, the first thing people think about when they hear that I am from Chicago is the murder rate. I don't want that to be the reputation of our city. Every week some teenager has been shot. This is not good. But the believers who live in Chicago can change it if we pray. That's why we have prayer, deliverance, and prophetic ministry at my church every Tuesday night. It's not just another service; it's corporate prayer.

We believe that if we call on God, He will do something in our city. The Bible says, "Everyone who calls on the name of the LORD will be saved [or delivered]" (Joel 2:32, cf. Rom. 10:13). We believe that, so we call upon God. We bind demons of murder, violence, guns, and shootings. We can't be a church in Chicago and just sit back, watch the news, and say, "Oh, my goodness. Things are so terrible." No. We can do something about this situation, because

God has given us power and authority: "Look, I give you authority to trample on serpents and scorpions, and over all the power of the enemy," He said. "And nothing shall by any means hurt you" (Luke 10:19).

I thank God for power and authority over serpents, scorpions, and all demonic powers. This is what the church should be about, not, "Rapture me, Lord. Get me out of here. Let me escape. Calgon, take me away." God is not Calgon.

I love the name of a church I preached for in the British Virgin Islands. It is called Transformation Church. I like that because they believe God is going to transform their communities and their nation through prayer. They also believe their prayers will give them strategy and wisdom to know how to get involved in business, politics, education, and other spheres of the culture they feel called to. They do prayer walks, get involved in politics, and teach their children how to start businesses. They are truly stewarding the glory of God that is being released in their region. We have the power to do the same.

We have to stop letting the devil take over. He is a liar and a bully. The way you deal with a bully is by standing up to him. The moment you run from a bully, you'll be running all your life. He'll take your lunch money, your cheese sandwich, your bologna sandwich, your turkey salad, your chicken salad, and your tuna salad. He'll start ordering stuff and putting it on your account: "Tomorrow, I want chicken salad." But the moment you stand up and say, "No, I'm not giving up my chicken salad. I'm eating today," the bully won't try you again because you stood up to him.

You Are Anointed to Throw the Enemy Down

God did not give the earth to the devil. He gave it to the children of man. We have the authority. We have the power—through prayer, prophecy, preaching, and teaching—to change things.

Intercessors and prophets have always changed history. Daniel changed history. Elijah changed history; he spent a great deal of his life fighting against Jezebel. And when Elijah left, God sent Jehu to deal with her. In 2 Kings 9:30–37 we read that Jehu didn't come to negotiate with Jezebel. He didn't come to fellowship with her. He came to kill her. I imagine him saying, "Enough of you. You have brought too much harm, destruction, witchcraft, and evil ideology to this nation. It is over." And the thing is, he was anointed to do it.

> The prophet poured the oil on Jehu's head and declared, "This is what the Lord, the God of Israel, says: 'I anoint you king over the Lord's people Israel. You are to destroy the house of Ahab your master, and I will avenge the blood of my servants the prophets and the blood of all the Lord's servants shed by Jezebel.... Dogs will devour her on the plot of ground at Jezreel, and no one will bury her.'"
>
> —2 Kings 9:6–10, niv

He did just as the Lord commanded:

> Then Jehu went to Jezreel. When Jezebel heard about it, she put on eye makeup, arranged her hair

> and looked out of a window. As Jehu entered the gate, she asked, "Have you come in peace, you Zimri, you murderer of your master?"
>
> He looked up at the window and called out, "Who is on my side? Who?" Two or three eunuchs looked down at him. "Throw her down!" Jehu said. So they threw her down, and some of her blood spattered the wall and the horses as they trampled her underfoot.
>
> —2 Kings 9:30–33, NIV

There was always somebody to stand up to Jezebel. There is always somebody who will throw her down. The spirit of Jezebel is one of many demonic powers at work in our day and age, and you have been anointed to throw down all the works of the enemy. Because you are anointed, when you show up and say, "Throw him down," he is coming down. You do not have to run and hide or let somebody else deal with him. You can deal with the enemy. You can announce to him that his days of deceiving, stealing, killing, and destroying are over. Throw him down.

Somebody has to stand up and do something. Somebody has to say, as Elijah did, "How long will you stay between two opinions? If the Lord is God, follow Him" (1 Kings 18:21). Somebody has to say, "The God that answers by fire, let Him be God" (v. 24). Somebody has to stand up and confront the prophets of Jezebel and of Baal. Somebody has to bind witchcraft and death and destruction and murder and poverty and injustice. Somebody has to do something. Are you bold enough to accept the fact that God has anointed you to be that somebody? Are you bold enough to accept the responsibility to pray and humble yourself before God?

I can hear God saying, "It's time to take care of some stuff. It's been going on too long. It's time to take care of things that have not been taken care of." This is His call to you. It's time for you to step up and do something about it. Will you take up the mantle of authority in the earth? Will you pray desperate prayers for the kingdom to advance and God's glory to spread to the ends of the earth? If so, I want you to join me in decreeing and declaring the follow prayers. Then in the next chapter we are going deeper into what effect the prayers of the saints have on the desperate times we are facing in our lives and in the earth. We are going to look at what happens in heaven when we pray.

Prayers That Change Things

Thank You, Lord, for returning to Your people dominion and authority over the earth.

Thank You for giving me power and authority over serpents, scorpions, and all demonic powers.

I thank You that my prayers make a difference.

I thank You, Lord, that You have given me the boldness and courage to take back my life, my family, my city, and my nation. I will not resign any of it to the enemy.

I accept my authority and responsibility as a believer to pray.

I shut the mouth of the enemy, who seeks to fill my head with lies that I am helpless, that my prayers have no effect, and that nothing will change.

I declare that the prayers of the righteous avail much (James 5:16).

I believe that when I pray in faith, mountains move.

I believe that when I pray, strongholds are broken.

I believe that when I pray, territories and regions are transformed.

I recommit myself to pray for the things that need to be changed in my world. I will be that someone who will stand up against the enemy and say, "Enough is enough." The devil will not take over.

I declare that the enemy be thrown down in the name of Jesus. I bind all his works to deceive, steal, kill, and destroy.

I bind witchcraft, death, destruction, murder, poverty, injustice, and any other thing that tries to stop the flow of God's glory in the earth.

Prayers That Move Mountains[2]

I speak to every mountain in my life and command it to be removed and cast into the sea (Mark 11:23).

I speak to every financial mountain to be removed from my life in the name of Jesus.

Let every evil mountain hear the voice of the Lord and be removed (Mic. 6:2).

I prophesy to the mountains and command them to hear the word of the Lord and be removed (Ezek. 36:4).

Let the mountains tremble at the presence of God (Hab. 3:10).

I contend with every mountain and command them to hear my voice (Mic. 6:1).

Lay the mountain of Esau (the flesh) to waste (Mal. 1:3).

Put forth Your hand, O Lord, and overturn the mountains by the roots (Job 28:9).

I speak to every mountain of debt to be removed and cast into the sea.

Lord, You are against every destroying mountain (Jer. 51:25).

Let the mountains melt at Your presence, O God (Judg. 5:5, KJV).

Make waste the evil mountains in my life, O Lord (Isa. 42:15).

I thresh every mountain, I beat them small, and I make the hills as chaff (Isa. 41:15).

Every mountain in my way will become a plain (Zech. 4:7).

Prayers of Humility[3]

Lord, I am humble. Guide me in justice and teach me Your ways (Ps. 25:9).

I will humble myself in the sight of the Lord, and He will lift me up (James 4:10).

I will not allow pride to enter my heart and cause me shame. I will be humble and clothed in wisdom (Prov. 11:2).

Lord, You take pleasure in me. You beautify me with salvation because I am humble (Ps. 149:4).

Lord, You will look on everyone who is proud, and You will humble them (Job 40:11).

Lord, You will save me (Ps. 18:27).

I will retain honor (Prov. 29:23).

I am better off being of a humble spirit with the lowly than dividing the spoil with the proud (Prov. 16:19).

I will humble myself under the mighty hand of God, that He may exalt me in due time (1 Pet. 5:6).

My soul will make its boast in the Lord. The humble will hear of it and be glad (Ps. 34:2).

I will see what God has done and be glad. Because I seek God, my heart will live (Ps. 69:32).

I will not be like Amon, but I will humble myself before the Lord and will not trespass more and more (2 Chron. 33:23).

I will remove my turban and take off my crown and let nothing be the same. I will exalt the humble and humble the exalted (Ezek. 21:26).

I am in the midst of a meek and humble people, and they will trust in the name of the Lord (Zeph. 3:12).

I will increase my joy in the Lord. I will rejoice in the Holy One of Israel (Isa. 29:19).

Like Daniel, I will not fear, because I know that from the first day I set my heart to understand Your ways and to humble myself before You, You heard my words and have come to me (Dan. 10:12).

Lord, humble me and test me, that I might do good in the end (Deut. 8:16).

I proclaim a fast right here that I might humble myself before my God to seek from Him the right way for me and my children and all of my possessions (Ezra 8:21).

My God will humble me among His people, and I will mourn for many who have sinned before and have not repented of the uncleanness, fornication, and lewdness that they have practiced (2 Cor. 12:21).

Lord, You said that if I humble myself, pray, and seek Your face and turn from my wicked ways, then You will hear from heaven and will forgive my sin and heal my land. Lord, I will do as You have commanded (2 Chron. 7:14).

Lord, You will dwell with him who has a contrite and humble spirit. You will revive the spirit of the humble and the hearts of the contrite ones. Let me be as they are (Isa. 57:15).

I will remember that the Lord my God led me all the way, even in the wilderness, to humble me and test me, to know what was in my heart, whether I would keep His commandments or not (Deut. 8:2).

God, You give more grace. You resist the proud but give grace to the humble (James 4:6).

Let me be like Moses, who was very humble, more than all the men who were on the face of the earth (Num. 12:3).

Lord, You do not forget the
cry of the humble (Ps. 9:12).

Arise, O Lord! O God, lift up Your hand!
Do not forget the humble (Ps. 10:12).

I will not set my mind on high things, but I will associate with the humble. I will not be wise in my own opinion (Rom. 12:16).

I will not pervert the way of the humble (Amos 2:7).

Lord, You have heard the desire of the humble. You will prepare their heart. You will cause Your ear to hear (Ps. 10:17).

I will submit myself to my elders. I will be clothed in humility, and God will give me grace (1 Pet. 5:5).

By humility and the fear of the Lord are
riches, honor, and life (Prov. 22:4).

I will speak evil of no one. I will be peaceable and
gentle, showing all humility to all men (Titus 3:2).

In humility I will correct those who are in opposition,
and perhaps God will grant them repentance so
that they may know the truth (2 Tim. 2:25).

The fear of the Lord is the instruction of wisdom,
and before honor is humility (Prov. 15:33).

Before destruction the heart of a man is haughty,
and before honor is humility (Prov. 18:12).

As the elect of God, holy and beloved, I will
put on tender mercies, kindness, humility,
meekness, and longsuffering (Col. 3:12).

I will seek the Lord. I will seek righteousness
and humility so that I may be hidden in
the day of the Lord's anger (Zeph. 2:3).

I take on the yoke of Christ, learning from Him,
for He is meek and lowly in heart (Matt. 11:29).

I will do what the Lord requires of me:
I will do justly, love mercy, and walk
humbly with my God (Mic. 6:8).

I desire to be like Christ, who humbled Himself
and became obedient to the point of death,
even the death of the cross (Phil. 2:8).

Lord, I have humbled myself; please do not
bring calamity upon me (1 Kings 21:29).

Through humility and the fear of the Lord I am
given riches and honor and life (Prov. 22:4).

The Lord regards the lowly (Ps. 138:6).

I will humble myself as a little child (Matt. 18:4).

Chapter 8

The Prayers of the Saints

> Another angel, having a golden censer, came and stood at the altar. He was given much incense to offer with the prayers of all the saints on the golden altar which was before the throne. The smoke of the incense, with the prayers of the saints, ascended before God from the angel's hand.
>
> —Revelation 8:3–4

The Book of Revelation is about the prayers of the saints causing a release of the purposes of God in the earth. In Revelation 8, the saints were praying as they were taught to pray: "Thy kingdom come. Thy will be done." (See Matthew 6:7–13.) You may be wondering why they needed to pray that way. Why couldn't the kingdom just come? Well, in Revelation 12–18 there is also a picture of the dragon, the beast, and the false prophet. There's a picture of Babylon. There is also a picture of wickedness, which is there for one reason: to prevent God's kingdom from arriving.

Satan himself was and still is attempting to stop this kingdom from being established and coming into the hands of the saints as Jesus intended. During the time when the Gospels and Revelation were being written and distributed, the saints were being persecuted, killed, and put in prison.

They were going through a terrible time of tribulation. The dragon, which is in chapter 12, released a flood to try to kill the remnant of Christ's seed, which was Abraham's seed (v. 15–17; see also Gal. 3:29). Satan did not want the kingdom of God to be established and to advance, so he fought. He persecuted. He killed. He caused wickedness to increase. But it was the prayers of the saints that caused God to act.

In Revelation 8 we get a picture of what happened in the spirit at that time when the saints would pray. An angel took those prayers and lifted them to heaven. Those prayers came up before God, and the angel then took those prayers, put them in a censer, and cast them to the earth (v. 5). When the angel cast the prayers to the earth, earthquakes, thundering, and lightning erupted, which is a picture of judgment. The things that stood in the way of the kingdom advancing were dealt with—the dragon, the beast, the false prophet, and Babylon. Every evil that stood in the way of God's people was judged and brought to its end.

My premise here is simply this: whatever is standing in your way, when you learn how to pray, the justice, judgment, and vengeance of the Lord are released against it, and His purpose in your life and the lives of those for whom you pray is established and can once again advance.

The Justice, Judgment, and Vengeance of God

The Book of Revelation is also a book about justice. One of the major themes of this book is the vengeance of God.

It was prophesied by Moses in Deuteronomy 32:35:

> Vengeance is Mine, and recompense; their foot will slip in due time; for the day of their calamity is at hand, and the things to come hasten upon them.

Jesus talked about it in Matthew 23:31–36:

> Therefore you are witnesses against yourselves that you are sons of those who murdered the prophets. Fill up, then, the measure of your fathers' guilt.
>
> You serpents! You generation of vipers! How can you escape the judgment of hell? Therefore I send you prophets, and wise men, and scribes. Some of them you will kill and crucify, and some you will scourge in your synagogues and persecute them from city to city, that on you may come all the righteous blood shed on the earth, from the blood of righteous Abel to the blood of Zechariah son of Berekiah, whom you murdered between the temple and the altar. Truly I say to you, all these things will come on this generation.

It is mentioned in Revelation 6:10:

> How long, O Sovereign Lord, holy and true, until You judge and avenge our blood on those who dwell on the earth?

And again in Revelation 18:20–21:

> "Rejoice over her, O heaven and saints and apostles and prophets, for God has avenged you against her."
>
> Then a mighty angel took up a stone like a great millstone and threw it into the sea, saying: "With

> such violence shall that great city Babylon be thrown down, and shall be found no more."

One of the things that really upsets most of us more than anything else is injustice. We hate it. And one of the worst things that happens with injustice is that even though we see it, it often seems as if there is very little we can do about it. Whether there is an unjust leader or an evil system that is so big—it could be racism, communism, fascism, witchcraft, or any system in place that you see is wrong—it's easy to feel helpless when you're staring down both the injustice and the way it is impacting people's lives. Some of us know firsthand how it is to be part of a group that is oppressed by a large, evil system. Have you ever questioned, "What can I do? I'm just a nobody. I don't have a title or position. I can't change the laws or do anything to turn this around. No one listens to me. They won't even let me in the building. If they have a hearing, they'll cut the mic off before I get a chance to speak." So often we find ourselves in positions like this, where the solutions don't seem to be in our hands, and that feeling of helplessness makes it worse. These are some of the desperate times and situations we've been talking about.

From Nobodies to Praying Saints

If you remember how the church began and grew out of those one hundred twenty saints in the Upper Room, then you'll also recall that they were up against a rigid religious and political system. They too may have felt at times that the unjust systems and leaders they faced were too big to change, but they persevered in prayer and never stopped sharing the true testimony of Christ. They remained faithful and obedient to Jesus's last instructions before leaving earth (Acts 1:4–8) and waited for the power of the Holy Spirit to fall on them (Acts 2:1–3). One hundred twenty faithful ones were filled with the Holy Ghost, and they became five thousand.

However, their testimony of Christ was in opposition to what the religious leaders wanted to promote, and they found themselves being persecuted. (See Acts 4.) Stephen was killed (Acts 7:54–60). John the Baptist's head was cut off (Matt. 14:10). Peter was put in prison (Acts 12:3–19). Everywhere the apostle Paul went, he was beaten and thrown in prison (Acts 16:16–40; 28:16–31; 2 Cor. 11:23–27). Yet the saints prayed for both Peter and Paul, and they were released from their bonds.

The saints at this time were called Nazarenes after Jesus of Nazareth. Nazareth was a city in Galilee, and the Galileans were considered country bumpkins, if you will. Jerusalem had the city slickers. Nazareth was so bad that Nathanael said, "Can any good thing come out of Nazareth?" (John 1:46). It was a city where nobody who was anybody came from. It was an unknown place. Yet these people who were called Nazarenes were following this Nazarene guy, Jesus, a nobody. They were all despised nobodies. They were not elite. Some of them were not from Jerusalem and had no seminary education, no degrees. Most of the closest followers of Jesus were Galileans, fishermen from the poorest, darkest, lowest area in the region.

This is where Jesus came from as well, which made it easier for the religious leaders to put Him and His followers in prison, cut their heads off, and persecute, torture, and torment them. They were seen as nobodies, but they knew how to do one thing: they knew how to pray. Jesus taught them that. (See Matthew 6:7–13.)

If you don't learn anything else in life, learn how to pray. If you don't learn Greek and Hebrew, learn how to pray. When you know how to pray, no weapon formed against you will prosper. When you know how to call upon God and pray, you are somebody. I don't care how much of a nobody people say you are. With prayer, you are somebody to God. Prayer is your greatest weapon. Prayer makes you somebody in the kingdom. That small, despised, and persecuted group of nobodies, those Nazarenes—they knew how to pray. They knew how to call upon God. They knew how to pray despite what they were up against. Even as the persecution intensified and they were pressed on every side, they knew how to pray until chains were shaken loose and prison doors were opened.

> About midnight Paul and Silas were praying and singing hymns to God, and the other prisoners were listening to them. Suddenly there was such a violent earthquake that the foundations of the prison were shaken. At once all the prison doors flew open, and everyone's chains came loose.
>
> —Acts 16:25–26, NIV

Earthquake Prayers

Sometimes when you pray, it looks like the situation gets bigger and the systems of oppression seem like they will never fall. Keep praying. You will fall right into the devil's plan if you stop. A time is coming when your prayers will join with the prayers of others. A time is coming when God will say, "OK, it is enough. Angels, get those prayers and release them in the earth." Once those prayers are released, you are going to see thunder, lightning, and earthquakes. Things are going to begin to shake in the realm that you've been praying about.

Your prayers cause earthquakes—and as you have probably already figured out, I'm not talking about natural earthquakes. When you pray, stuff starts shaking—stuff that was standing strong, laughing, mocking, and talking about you. All of a sudden, whatever foundation these evil systems propped themselves up on will begin to shake.

When you pray, God will shake up every ungodly, wicked system that stands in your way. Earthquakes and, as Revelation 8:5 declares, the thunder of God will be released. Let God thunder in the heavens for you. Let the lightning of God come. Let the earthquakes of God come. Let the voice of God come into your situation, your land, and your city. God, let the systems of this world be shaken up. Let the thunder of God clap against the works of hell.

Babylon falls, Satan is bound, the kingdom of God advances, the new heaven and the new earth come, and the river of God flows—all because somebody prayed. This is what the Book of Revelation teaches us. Saints prayed, "Thy kingdom come. Thy will be done," and their prayers released a chain of events. It's almost as if prayer sometimes has to hit a tipping point; once it fills up the censers in heaven, God releases it, and a domino effect takes place. Wicked systems, people, and places start falling all over the place. And all of a sudden, God begins to release His angels, and they blow the trumpets, pour out the bowls, and release fire and judgments. Then new things begin to come. What was in heaven begins to come down to earth. What was far away begins to come near. The river of God begins to flow, and revival comes. This is all the result of prayer.

When we get a revelation of the power of our prayers, and we begin to pray corporately, believing God that our prayers really do make a difference, it's time for revival. When we begin to petition God with prayers like, "Lord, let Your kingdom advance in this region. Let salvation come. Let strength come. Let Your kingdom come. Let the accuser of the brethren be cast down. Let the works of hell be destroyed. Father, let what the enemy has been doing come to an end," it's time for God's glory to come and fill the earth.

Out With the Old and In With the New

I love the Book of Revelation because it is not just a book about the end of an age. It is also a book about the beginning of something new—a new heaven and a new earth. God ends the old so that He can release the new. In essence God tells the devil, "All this old stuff you've been doing—accusing, persecuting, holding My people down, holding them back, and wearing them out—it's ending. I am going to create a new heaven and a new earth. All that old stuff is passed away." As the Bible says, "Therefore, if any man is in Christ, he is a new creature. Old things have passed away. Look, all things have become new" (2 Cor. 5:17).

Your breakthrough is here. You've been praying and praying and praying, and you didn't just start praying today. You've been praying, like Hannah, month after month, year after year. God has been collecting those prayers. It is time for the release, and it will come like a tsunami in the spirit. That is why we need long-term saints who won't pray for two months and quit when they don't see breakthrough right away. The things God wants to release in the earth are major. The saints are not praying for little miracles. We are believing for our cities and states to be turned around. We are believing for America and the nations of the world to be opened up. We are praying for what is loosed in heaven to be loosed on the earth. We are praying for a new level of kingdom advancement and increase.

Saints and the House of Prayer

> Also the sons of the foreigner who join themselves to the LORD to serve Him, and to love the name of the LORD, and to be His servants, to everyone who keeps from polluting the Sabbath and takes hold of My covenant, even them I will bring to My holy mountain and make them joyful in My house of prayer. Their burnt offerings and their sacrifices shall be accepted on My altar; for My house shall be called a house of prayer for all people.
>
> —ISAIAH 56:6–7

Isaiah 56:6–7 is one of my favorite passages on the subject of prayer. It talks about God bringing us to the holy mountain. The holy mountain is the place of God's rule, authority, power, presence, and glory. The mountain of God is also the house of God. However, under the new covenant it is not a physical place but the place of prayer in the spirit. We are now the temple (1 Cor. 6:19), the house of God. The house of God is a corporate people. It is a gathering of the saints of God. It is a spiritual house made up of living stones. It is not made up of physical stones. Remember, the old covenant temple was just a type of something greater. The natural was a type or picture of the spiritual. The new covenant temple is the church, the house of God. We are the temple of God, yes, but the corporate gathering of the saints is also the house of God.

Notice Isaiah 56:7 says that as we come to this house, we come with joy. God makes us joyful in His house. Now this is a tremendous word because it tells us that it should be natural for us not only to pray but also to enjoy prayer. It should be something that flows out of us, something that is not difficult or that we have to struggle with. God actually makes us joyful in the house of prayer. In other words, we come with excitement, joy, and happiness because of God's mercy.

Another thing to note is that these verses are talking about the stranger or the foreigner coming into the house of prayer. When you study the Old Testament temple, the only people who could actually go into the temple were Jewish men. Women could not go inside the temple. There was a court outside the temple called the Court of the Women.[1] There was another court called the Court of the Gentiles.[2] A Gentile, or non-Jewish person, could not go into the house of God because Gentiles were uncircumcised and considered unclean. But now that the new covenant has come, God has eliminated those barriers. The house of prayer is open to all.

I remember when my team and I went to Israel and we prayed at the Western Wall. Still today, men are the only people who can go inside the temple. Women have a separate place outside a fence. When we went in, the women on our team had to stand on the other side of the fence. They were upset and asked, "Apostle, what is this?" That experience was so unfamiliar to us because women in my ministry are used to being a part of praise and worship and prayer.

As new covenant believers, we don't have these separations anymore. Religious systems always put up barriers, setting up hierarchies with one group up here and another group down here. God did call Israel to be a separate nation under the old covenant. So there were strangers, foreigners, and outsiders who had no covenant with God. But in this passage in Isaiah 56, God is speaking of a day when these strangers would no longer be strangers in the house of God. They would joyfully come from every nation, people, tribe, and tongue.

Prayer is special; don't lose appreciation for it.

In Matthew 21 something interesting happens in the house of God. Evidently the house God gave Israel had become a den of thieves by the time Jesus came. In verse 12 we find Him in the temple beating out the money changers and driving out thieves. It seems that Israel didn't really appreciate the house of God the way they should have. Instead of it being a house of prayer as God intended, they allowed it to become a place to buy and sell and transact even shady business. They were not enjoying God, and He was not enjoying them.

What stood out to me in this instance was that when you don't appreciate something, God will take it from you and give it to somebody who does. You can have something so special but take it for granted. When you had it, you abused it, neglected it, took advantage of it, mistreated it, and ignored it. But the people without it, when they get it, are so excited to have it.

It's easy to forget how special it is that, first, we are temples where the presence of God can dwell and, second, that we can join with others on the mountain of God, in the house of prayer, to speak to God and hear Him speak to us. Making our requests known to Him and then hearing His plans and purposes for our lives is so exciting when we first come into it. Now some of us are basically yawning and saying, "Yeah, I've been in this for ten years." Some of us have lost our joy, zeal, and appreciation for it. If we feel like this when it comes to prayer, we must realize that this was also where Jesus found Israel when He came into the temple that day.

He let them know that a day was coming when He was going to open His house of prayer to the whole world. What had been exclusively set up in Jerusalem would no longer be the place of worship and prayer. Jesus confirmed this when He told the woman, "The hour is coming when neither on this mountain nor in Jerusalem will you worship the Father.... Yet the hour is coming, and is now here, when the true worshippers will worship the Father in spirit and truth" (John 4:21–23).

Prayer Moves Heaven and Earth

God is opening up His house of prayer so that it surpasses natural limitations. Obviously, the whole world cannot fit within the physical city limits of Jerusalem. God is opening up His house of prayer to hold something heavenly, something bigger than an earthly city or nation. He's opening it up to hold something that is big enough to handle Africa, Asia, Europe, North America, South America, Australia, and the islands of the sea. He's opening it up to something that is big enough to handle everybody's prayer. And that place is called heavenly Jerusalem. If you don't already know it, let me tell you: the heavenly realm is bigger than the earthly realm. This is what He really means by the coming of the kingdom of heaven. This is what real kingdom living is all about. This is when heaven touches earth.

Kingdom living is joyful prayer. What we call prayer in some of our churches today is not prayer. There is no joy, strength, or fire. People are sad and defeated to the point where they make it hard for anyone to want to even pray. Sometimes in these settings we are glad when prayer is over. That is not kingdom prayer.

True prayer, effectual prayer, the prayer of the saints, comes from people who are full of joy, excitement, expectation, and faith, knowing the greatness and majesty of whom they pray to. Because of this, they are ready to pray. They are glad to come into the house of the Lord to pray His will and His glory into the earth. They understand the power of the kingdom. They understand the fullness of the salvation Jesus came to bring to people's lives. They understand God's plan to fill the earth with His glory, and they understand that prayer is what makes it happen.

We should not have to be forced or pressured into praying. And when we do gather, it should not be normal for there to be little evidence of the presence of God. It should not be normal that there is no glory, joy, praise, worship, shouting, and dancing. We should not see it as normal for people to come into the house of prayer and be bored and not want to pray or open their mouths. We should not be able to sit there looking at our watches or texting on our phones, not if we understand what it means to be the saints of God whose prayers move heaven and earth.

Saints know that prayer is too special to be treated as something regular. We know that it is OK to launch out into the deep in prayer. It is OK to show excitement when coming into the presence of God with our requests and petitions, honor and reverence, praise and worship. It is OK to show our zeal and passion for the Lord. It is OK to come before the Lord with great expectations. It is OK to enjoy God and to know that when we pray, He hears our prayers and answers them. Our prayers have a great impact, both in heaven and on earth. Don't hold back. Pray with power so that the earth shakes, the thunder claps, the lightning of God strikes, and every plan and purpose of God becomes established on earth as it is in heaven.

Earthquake Prayers That Release God's Justice

Father, I thank You for the mighty and great things being released to Your church. Thank You, Lord, for miracles, revival, and breakthrough.

Let the powers of hell be broken. Let Babylon fall down. Let the accuser of the brethren be shut up. Let the dragon be bound, in the name of Jesus.

Let new heavens and a new earth come, Father. Let new things come, in the name of Jesus.

Lord, I believe my prayers make a difference. I have power through prayer.

Lord, I believe Your Word when You say, "Call to Me, and I will answer you, and show you great and mighty things" (Jer. 33:3). I believe that "everyone who calls on the name of the Lord shall be saved" (Rom. 10:13). So, Lord, I call upon the name of Jesus for salvation, healing, and deliverance. I call upon You, O God, to release the prayers of the saints in the earth. Release an earthquake. Release Your thunder. Release Your lightning. Release Your fire. Release Your power. Release Your judgment, in the name of Jesus.

Let justice come, and let every corrupt system fall.

Let those who are oppressed by the systems of this world be loosed from the powers that bind them, in the name of Jesus.

Release Your vengeance on the principalities and powers that rule in high places.

Let wicked leaders be exposed and, if they don't repent, let them be removed from their positions. Let righteous leaders arise and take their place.

Let wicked social, political, religious, and economic systems be destroyed. Let justice and righteousness take their place.

Turn our cities, states, nations, and world around, O God. Let the wicked be removed out of their place. Let Your glory put to death anything that is not holy as You are holy.

Lord, I call upon You in the midnight hour.

Lord, let Your kingdom come.

Let the saints pray and not lose heart. Let us tarry, O God. Let us not give in to spiritual slumber. Let us stay awake and pray.

Let my prayers go to another level. Let my prayer life shift into a new dimension.

Hear and answer my prayers, O God, and bring miracles and breakthroughs into not only my life but into every dark and wicked place in the earth. Let Your justice reign.

Let everything in my way fall because of my prayers, in Jesus' name.

Lord, I release Your grace, favor, and shalom over Your people. Do miracles for us, O God. Show Yourself strong on our behalf and in the earth.

Let every knee bow and every tongue confess that You are Lord and that Your kingdom reigns and has no end.

Prayers for National Deliverance

Lord, I thank You for deliverance.

Lord, I pray for deliverance to hit this nation, for devils to be cast out, for strongholds to be broken, for wickedness to be loosed, in the name of Jesus.

Lord, I pray for the power of the Holy Ghost to hit this nation.

Along with the saints who are praying even now, God, I come against the demons of perversion, racism, poverty, anger, and violence. I bind them in the name of Jesus. I pray that their assignments over our generation and the generations to come be broken in the name of Jesus.

Lord, I pray that You would save, heal, and deliver those who are overcome by these demons and those who have been their victims, in the name of Jesus.

I pray for the judges, lawmakers, and other justice workers, in the name of Jesus, that they will make righteous and fair judgments.

Father, I pray for a mighty power of deliverance to sweep my church and my nation. I pray that Your deliverance will come to Your global church and all the nations of the earth, in the name of Jesus.

God, I pray for preachers who do not cast out devils. Lord, let them begin to cast out devils. Lord, I pray for pastors who do not deal in deliverance. We pray that you will deliver them, O God, from demons of religion and tradition. Set in their hearts a righteous indignation toward injustice and the oppression of Your people. Increase their love and compassion for those who are oppressed by the devil.

Lord, I pray for religious leaders who are not leading Your people righteously. Open their eyes to their own injustices. Empower them by Your Spirit to repent and be delivered.

In the name of Jesus, Lord, I bind the spirit of compromise. I pray for Holy Ghost conviction to come. I pray for holiness to return to the house of God. I pray for righteousness to return to the church. I pray for it to be in our churches. I pray for the power of God to manifest in our churches. In the name of Jesus, I bind every lying devil and demon of deception that would cause people to think that bondage is normal and they are helpless against it.

Lord, I pray that a new spirit of prayer will sweep through the body of Christ.

Father, I thank You for salvation and deliverance coming to my country. I pray for revival to come to the church.

Let the rivers of living water flow from my belly.

Let the hand that delivers be released.

Let the hand of God come upon us.

Let the sword of the Lord cut asunder every work of darkness to break the chains, ropes, and fetters of iron. I break them and rebuke them in the name of Jesus.

I rebuke every unclean devil that is loose in my nation. I bind you in the name of Jesus.

I declare that my nation is not evolving into unrighteousness. It is moving toward righteousness, in the name of Jesus.

Prayers for Recommitment to the House of Prayer

Heavenly Father, I recommit myself to the house of prayer for all nations.

Lord, You have brought me to Your mountain and made me joyful in the house of prayer. I will enjoy the house of prayer, and I will take my place in it.

I drive out prayerlessness, laziness, slothfulness, lukewarmness, and apathy. Let a fresh wind of prayer blow into our church. I believe it and I receive it, in Jesus' name.

Chapter 9

Then Comes Revival

> And Josiah was eight years old when he began to reign, and he was king for thirty-one years in Jerusalem....And in the eighth year of his reign, while he was still a young boy, he began to seek out the God of David his father; and in the twelfth year he began to cleanse Judah and Jerusalem from high places, Asherah poles, idols, and carved and cast images.
>
> —2 CHRONICLES 34:1–3

REVIVAL IS NEEDED during desperate times. The injustice and social issues we see create the urgency needed to stir up a spirit of prayer within the body of Christ. When saints pray and seek God, He will show us what needs to be purged in order to bring revival and restoration to our lives and communities. The reign of King Josiah, recorded in 2 Chronicles 34 and 35, gives us a pattern for seeing revival, renewal, and restoration come into our most desperate situations.

In order to get the appropriate setting for the environment in which Josiah became king, we need to look briefly at the reign of the kings who came before him—his father, grandfather, and great-grandfather. I'll start with his great-grandfather, Hezekiah. Hezekiah was a godly king who, if you will recall, became ill and asked the Lord to extend his life. God granted his request, and Hezekiah ruled righteously for the rest of his life, bringing revival back to the land. But then after Hezekiah died, his son Manasseh (Josiah's grandfather) came into power.

Manasseh was one of the wickedest kings Israel ever had. (See 2 Chronicles 33.) He had the longest reign—fifty-five years—during which he led Israel into all kinds of idolatry, witchcraft, sorcery, and divination. As a judgment against him, God had the king of Babylon come and take Manasseh from his throne in Jerusalem and put him in prison in Babylon. While he was in prison, Manasseh repented because he recognized he had messed up, and God restored him to his throne in Jerusalem.

Manasseh's story is one of the most amazing accounts in the Bible of an individual who was involved in all kinds of witchcraft and divination but repented. The Bible says he humbled himself, and God brought him out of prison and restored him to his throne in Jerusalem. When he died, his son Amon took over the throne.

Amon was also an evil king. (See 2 Chronicles 33:21–25.) He only reigned for two years before his servants conspired against him and killed him. After they murdered him, the people of the land caught everyone who conspired against Amon, killed them, and made Josiah their new king.

When Josiah ascended the throne, he was only eight years old. His father had just been murdered, so he was coming into a pretty bad situation. Being so young, he probably had someone helping him to rule the kingdom. Immediately he got on track to become one of Israel's greatest godly kings. He was responsible for repairing the house of God, which had been in disrepair and neglected. He restored the Passover to the land, the priesthood back to its purpose, and praise and worship back into the house of God. He was also responsible for rediscovering the Law of God, which had been completely lost.

Josiah's reign is a model for how revival and restoration of the land—the earth—starts with the people of God. That is why this message of what to pray and what to expect in desperate times is so important. We are in a time of desperation in our world. What is evil is being called good; what is good is being called evil. There are things in our lives that must be purged if desperate times are to give way to times of revival and glory. Let's take a closer look at the steps Josiah took to restore God's glory among his people, heal the desperation of their times, and usher in the last revival the people of Israel would see before their captivity in Babylon.

Purge the Land

> In the eighth year of his reign, while he was still a young boy, [Josiah] began to seek out the God of David his father; and in the twelfth year he began to cleanse Judah and Jerusalem from high places, Asherah poles, idols, and carved and cast images.
>
> So they tore down the altars for the Baals, and he cut down the incense altars that were above them and smashed the Asherah poles and carved and cast images. And he crushed them to dust and scattered them before the graves of those who sacrificed to them.
>
> —2 Chronicles 34:3–4

What's interesting about Josiah's beginning actions as king—and something we will find out later—is that this young man had no Book of the Law. That wasn't discovered until later. All of his actions at this point were based on his desire to seek God. And with that desire, God put in Josiah's heart the motivation to remove idols and images from throughout the territory. Josiah began with purging the land of Judah and the city of Jerusalem.

How do we apply this in our own lives?

Get rid of idols.

Josiah's story shows us that as we seek God, He will give us the desire to get rid of the ungodly things in our lives. As you seek God, you find Him. And as you come into His presence, conviction comes, and you begin to want to take on His image, which is holy. You are motivated to remove things from your life that separate you from God and His standard of holiness. A person who is seeking God for any period of time will begin to remove the idols and unclean things from her life. That's why you cannot tell me someone is truly seeking God and still holding on to idols. This purging is also a picture of deliverance.

See, we often want revival, but we don't want to get there God's way. We want to see a move of God in the land; we want peace and freedom in our lives; we want fulfillment of dreams; we want blessings; we want fruit, increase, and multiplication; but we don't want to seek God and begin to deal with the things in our lives that we place before God. But this is what should happen and what Josiah modeled for us during his reign in Israel.

Dig up the roots of generational bondage and sin and burn them.

> Then he burned the bones of the priests on their altars and so cleansed Judah and Jerusalem.
>
> —2 Chronicles 34:5

What Josiah did here may seem harsh or extreme, but the priests were false priests, and it shows the level of godly righteousness and zeal in this twenty-year-old man. He doesn't just deal with stuff in a nice way, which is a problem we have sometimes. We want to deal with the enemy and his devices in a nice way, but that is not how we break free. Sometimes it takes righteous zeal to tear down the idols and things in our lives and in our land that rise up against the knowledge of God. We can't just pat them down. Sometimes we have to cast them or throw them down.

So the Bible is telling us that Josiah began to break stuff down. He dug up the bones of the false priests—as if their control and false prophecies over the people were not dead enough—and burned their bones. It is as if he called the coroner's office and had their bones exhumed just to make sure every evil thing they led the people into was good and dead.

Josiah recognized that his city was defiled and unclean, that it needed to be cleaned up in honor of the God who had given them the land. He was dealing with the things every ungodly king before him brought into the land. He knew one of his own forefathers had led the people into rebellion and permitted all kinds of wickedness and evil. He was turning the tables and cleaning up strongholds and bondages that were generational.

We often talk about getting deliverance from generational

spirits. Some of the things that we battle have been introduced into our lives or our communities as a result of what our ancestors have done. It could be smoking, drinking, perversion, lust, uncleanness, drug addiction, witchcraft, or mishandling money and resources. However long those issues have been in your family, when you begin to seek God, He will give you the desire to get them out of your life, to be cleansed, to pray for revival to come, and to want His blessing to come upon your life. His Spirit will cause you to want to get rid of those things so you can have the fullness of God instead.

God will show you what to get rid of.

Sometimes when we sense that we've been far from God and begin to draw near, we may not know exactly what we need to get rid of to have more of Him in our lives. But as you do this, trust that God will lead you. I'm sure this is what happened in Josiah's case. He had no Scripture, and when he finally received a confirming word from the Lord through the prophetess Huldah, he was well into the purging process. She sent back a prophetic word to him, confirming that he was going in the right direction:

> Because your heart was tender and you humbled yourself before God when you heard His words against this place and those who dwell here, and you have brought yourself low before Me and torn your clothes and wept before Me, I have heard you, declares the LORD. I am bringing you to be with your fathers, and you will be brought to your grave in peace, and your eyes will not see all the disaster

> that I am bringing on this place and on those who dwell here.
>
> —2 Chronicles 34:27–28

If you recall, in the account of Hannah, the prophet Eli didn't get involved in her story until the end. He confirmed that God had heard her prayers and would grant her request (1 Sam. 1:17). But she had been on her own with God for years and years before she had received a word from the prophet. During that time, we can conclude that Hannah remained faithful to the Lord. She pursued God first with her desire to have a child rather than giving in to worry or trying to manipulate things on her own to get what she wanted. Hannah went to God as her source, and because of that He was able to lead her, even before He intervened through Eli, and answer her prayer.

God will help you. He will show you what to do even if there isn't a prophet or prophetic word to get you started. But I also believe the prophetic is important for deliverance, restoration, and revival. Their primary function in the body of Christ is "to root out and to pull down, to destroy and to throw down, to build and to plant" (Jer. 1:10). So God will send a prophet at some point to help.

Therefore, don't despise when godly and prophetic people show up and begin to help you to cleanse. Sometimes we need them because we just don't know what to do. We're seeking God, and He is dealing with us. But one way He helps is by sending a godly person who will say, "This is not of God, and that's not of God. You need to get rid of this. You need to dig that up and burn it." If you want God to move in your life, you have to get rid of some stuff, and in His mercy, He will help you.

Digging up stuff is not always pleasant.

No, it won't always be pleasant to dig up some of the stuff God shows you. Can you imagine what it was like for the priests to dig up the remains of the false prophets? This is the unpleasant part of revival that we don't want to deal with. Some people just want to move right into the presence of God, but you just don't move right into the presence of God when you have a bunch of junk in your life. His glory will crush you.

In order to stand in revival under the weight of God's glory, you must have a clean and pure heart. This is the place Josiah was moving the people to. It's called repentance, renunciation, and deliverance. It is not pleasant, but it is necessary.

Some preachers today will tell you that you don't have to get rid of anything, that God loves and accepts you. It's all by grace. This is partly true. God does love you. He loves us all. But you can't have a bunch of unclean stuff in your life or in your land and expect the blessing of God and revival to come. The presence of God doesn't dwell among demons, sorcery and witchcraft, and perversion. That stuff has to come out.

Listen, we're trying to get the glory of God in our lives, right? We are tired of living without the fullness of His presence. We want to be revived and restored, right? This means we can't just live any kind of raggedy, unclean life. Let me make this clear as well: I am not talking about when you have a problem and you are already working toward being delivered. I am also not saying you have to be perfect and can never make a mistake. I'm talking about sinful lifestyles where people just accept it and call evil good, and good evil, where even if they are aware of their sin, they resign to do nothing about it. No, God has a standard of holiness and righteousness, and His glory will not abide in anything less.

Repair the House

> In the eighteenth year of his reign, when he had purged the land and the house, he sent Shaphan the son of Azaliah, Maaseiah the governor of the city, and Joah the son of Joahaz, the recorder, to repair the house of the LORD his God.
>
> —2 CHRONICLES 34:8

The second thing Josiah did after purging the land was repair the house of God. This is a significant next step because of what we've discovered so far about what the house of God represents. In the Old Testament, of course, the house of God was a physical place in Jerusalem. It was the place of worship and prayer. We see in Josiah's process that when we seek God and purge things out of our lives through deliverance and prayer, it's natural that we begin to go toward a place of worship. It has always been the will of God for us to worship, for us to access what Jacob saw at the place he called Bethel, the place where angels ascend and descend. (See Genesis 28:12–19.) The house of God is the gate of heaven. There, heaven's blessings come upon your life.

I believe what often hinders worship is that the people who seek to worship have not dealt with stuff in their lives. We want glorious worship. We want the heavens to come down. We want smoke to fill the building like a cloud. But sometimes we don't want to deal with the junk in our lives. However, true worship only comes out of a place of cleanliness and godliness.

The reason the house of God needed to be repaired was because it had fallen down as a result of sin and idolatry. It had to be repaired and built back up. We often come to this realization in our lives when we look at the condition of the world around us. We know that repentance and purging are needed. We know restoration and repair need to happen. So we begin cleaning things out based on our desire to seek God. Then the word of the Lord comes, and we receive truth and instruction about what to do next.

Recover Truth

> When they brought out the money that had been given to the house of the LORD, Hilkiah the priest found the Book of the Law of the LORD from Moses.
>
> —2 CHRONICLES 34:14

Can you imagine? Israel had gotten so far away from God that they lost their Bible. How do you lose the Law of God? How did they get to a place where a nation that God made covenant with has no idea they were missing the Law of God? How had they strayed so far away from God that even the priests who were supposed to teach the Law didn't know where it was and hadn't ever read it?

> Then Hilkiah said to Shaphan the scribe, "I have found the Book of the Law in the house of the LORD." And Hilkiah gave the book to Shaphan.
>
> —2 CHRONICLES 34:15

What he found was Deuteronomy, the second transmission of the Law of God, which lists the blessings and the curses that would result if God's people were faithful—or unfaithful—in keeping the covenant God made with them. When they got down to the curses—can you imagine hearing that for the first time?—Josiah tore his clothes and basically said, "My God, we're in trouble." This was the first time he had ever heard this.

Now, you have it in your Bible, and you can read it. As a matter of fact, you probably quote part of it as a decree or declaration: "I'm blessed coming in. I'm blessed going out. I'm the head and not the tail. I'm blessed in the city and blessed in the field." You've heard this before, but Josiah had not.

> Then the king ordered Hilkiah, Ahikam the son of Shaphan, Abdon the son of Micah, Shaphan the scribe, and Asaiah the attendant of the king: "Go and seek the Lord on my behalf and on the behalf of the remnant in Israel and Judah concerning what is written in the book that was found, for the wrath of the Lord that is poured out on us is great because our fathers have not kept the word of the Lord, to do everything that is written in this book."
>
> So Hilkiah and those with the king went to Huldah the prophetess.
>
> —2 Chronicles 34:20–22

Thank God for prophets. The king had the Word of God and didn't know what to do, so he sent for a prophet. In response, she sent back to him a word from the Lord telling him what was going to happen.

Another principle in this story that I want to show here is when you seek God, not only will it lead you to purge things and to come to a place of worship, but it also will lead you to discover truth that has been lost. Every time there is a move of God or revival, there is a recovery of certain truths that have somehow been lost. We lose certain truths because of neglect and sin, but in revival these truths are recovered because we are seeking God and beginning to restore gateways to His presence. For example, with the Azusa Street revival in the early 1900s, the rediscovered truth was the baptism of the Holy Spirit with the evidence of speaking in tongues. It is so important that we rediscover not only worship but also truth. Truth liberates. John 8:32 says, "You shall know the truth, and the truth shall set you free."

Revival is not just for you to feel good, shout, dance, get goose bumps, and fall out. Revival is restoration. Revival is worship. Revival is repairing the house of God. Revival is rediscovering truth through the Word of God and destroying ignorance. It brings so many blessings in your life. In revival you begin to walk in things that have been lost through years of neglect. When these things come to light, you can then respond to them by renewing your covenant with God.

Renew the Covenant

When Josiah heard the Book of Law, he didn't just take it for himself. He made sure the priests, Levites, and all the people, small and great, received its truths as well. He read the Word to them, and in 2 Chronicles 34:31 we see that he made a covenant with God:

> Then the king stood in his place and made a covenant before the LORD, to walk after the LORD, and to keep His commandments and His testimonies and His statutes with all his soul, to perform the words of the covenant written in this book.

Revival causes people to renew their commitment to God. Then notice verse 33:

> So Josiah took away all the detestable things from the lands that belonged to the people of Israel and caused all who were found in Israel to serve their LORD God. And all his days they did not turn away from the LORD God of their fathers.

After Josiah renewed the covenant with God, he went even further with what the move of God was stirring in his immediate area. He went into all the countries where the people of Israel lived and took away all the abominations.

Sometimes one deliverance is not enough. You can start cleaning yourself up and purging yourself, but the more you hear God's Word, get into the house of God, and recommit yourself to Him, the more you'll begin to purge and take away the things in your life that God shows you need to go.

Take Up a Josiah Anointing

> The singers, the sons of Asaph, were in their places according to the command of David, Asaph, Heman, and Jeduthun the king's seer. The gatekeepers were

> at each of the gates; they did not need to leave their service, for their brothers the Levites made preparations for them.
>
> —2 CHRONICLES 35:15

When it looks like everything has been lost, God will raise up Josiahs, reformers and apostolic men and women, to get back what was lost. These leaders guide us through the restoration process and help us purge things out of our lives, recommit ourselves to God, restore us to our place in the kingdom, and rebuild ministries. They initiate the cleansing process and break down strongholds. They preach the recovered word of truth and lead the processes of repairing, rebuilding, restoration, and recommitment to the Word of God. Worship is restored. The singers are back in their place, and all the things that had been lost over generations return.

Successfully reclaiming and restoring what was lost is dependent on leadership. The leader Josiah was anointed for the job. It truly takes an anointing like his to make this level of transformation happen. Josiah's anointing is a type of apostolic anointing. He was the king, which is a type of apostle, in that he dealt with things that had gotten out of order. Through his leadership the function and purpose of the temple were restored. They had worship again, and the Passover, priests, Word of the Lord, and singers were all restored to their former glory. Everything that had been lost was restored.

Notice the prophets were not bringing revival in this story. The king was. The king was setting things straight. In the way God appoints apostles to break down what is defiled and establish the righteousness of God, Josiah was called to break down iniquity and idolatry in his land.

Sometimes people have a hard time with a strong and bold apostolic anointing. They say, "He's too strong. He preaches too hard. He doesn't have any love." But we can't just be nice and smiling and loving with sin and idolatry that are keeping us from coming into true worship and revival. We can't afford never to rebuke, correct, or confront the witchcraft, lust, perversion, injustice, or oppression that comes against God and His people. We have to deal with the junk first before the house of God can be restored.

I guess when Josiah was digging up the priests' bones, the people were saying he didn't have any love. "Why are you digging up their bones and burning them? That's not love." But there's only one way to deal with demons. You have to pull them down. Attack them. Burn them up. Then you can go and repair the house of God. You can't even look at building worship when sin, rebellion, and disobedience are running rampant.

In so many churches people are saying, "Let's bring in worship." No, we're going to have mass deliverance first. We're going to cast out devils first. We cannot worship God with idols in the land. In the new covenant, we are a holy priesthood, we are prophetic people, and we are all ministers of God. Some of us have a Josiah anointing, and we can take up the responsibility to be the ones who will lead the housecleaning in our own lives first and then strategically move out into our churches so that as a body we can affect our communities.

The house of God should be a house of glory and a house of prayer, not a place of entertainment. But it takes a certain kind of leader who is willing to deal with the idols, covetousness, greed, lust, and perversion. All these idols represent certain spirits in the hearts of people. Strong apostolic leaders will preach the truth to the people, bring revival and restoration, and lead them back to rediscover all that has been lost.

Don't Let Revival Die

Josiah's reign is a great story, but it is also a sad one. It was the last move of God that Israel had. Right after Josiah died, Israel went right back down. The revival did not even last more than one generation. His sons led the people right back into idolatry, and then God brought the Babylonians and led Israel into captivity.

But God is such a God of mercy. After seventy years He brought them back from Babylon to rebuild the temple and restore them again.

God always wants to restore, repair, and rebuild His people. When we mess up, in His mercy God will always raise up people who will bring revival and glory. So our prayer for this generation is that God will raise up godly men and women who will bring revival back to the cities and churches of America and the nations of the world. Let our churches once again be filled with His power and glory. May God raise them up.

Perhaps you are a Josiah who's been hidden and God is calling you out to a leading position. Maybe your dry season is a season of pruning and purging so that there is nothing in the way of God manifesting His favor, glory, and blessing through you to be a blessing to others. I would dare to believe there are more Josiahs in our midst than we know. With what we are facing in the earth in this season, I would dare to believe that the Josiahs are coming. With them, revival is coming. I pray that as we see the signs we would be zealous enough to do whatever it takes to fan the flames, to see God's glory fill the earth. May we be the generation that does not let what was begun in previous generations die.

Persistently Seek God

When we seek God, He answers. When you seek God, it is not a waste of time. As you seek Him, you begin to set into motion a chain of events that can change people's lives forever. Sometimes the devil will try to discourage you, but the Bible says that God "is a rewarder of those who diligently seek Him" (Heb. 11:6). When you begin to study the Word, pray, worship, and deal with the stuff in your life that is not like Him, the devil is not going to make it easy. He will fight you. But if you press into the process, God will bless you and cause His glory to manifest.

Prayers of Repentance and Renunciation[1]

Lord, I repent in dust and ashes (Job 42:6).

I will repent so that I won't perish (Luke 13:3).

I repent for my wickedness and pray that the thoughts of my heart be forgiven me (Acts 8:22).

I will not tolerate the spirit of Jezebel in my life. I will not suffer anguish because of her adultery. I will repent and hold fast to what I have (Rev. 2:20–25).

Thank You, Lord, that my sins have been blotted out and times of refreshing have come from Your presence because I have repented and been converted (Acts 3:19).

Lord, I repent. Do not remove my lampstand from its place (Rev. 2:5).

I receive the gift of the Holy Spirit because I have repented and have been baptized (Acts 2:38).

Lord, I repent, for Your kingdom is at hand (Matt. 3:2).

Lord, I repent, that Your mighty works will be done in me (Matt. 11:20).

I will be zealous and repent because You love me and chasten me (Rev. 3:19).

I will turn to God and do the works befitting repentance (Acts 26:20).

I repent now, for You will not always overlook my ignorance (Acts 17:30).

The Assyrian will not be my king, because I willingly repent (Hosea 11:5).

I repent and believe in the gospel (Mark 1:1).

I repent now of my evil way and evil doings, that I may dwell in the land that the Lord has given to me and my fathers forever (Jer. 25:5).

I repent, Lord, and turn away from my idols and all my abominations (Ezek. 14:6).

Do not judge me, O Lord. I repent and turn from all my transgressions so that iniquity will not be my ruin (Ezek. 18:30).

I repent and make supplication to You, Lord, saying, "I have sinned and done wrong. I have committed wickedness" (1 Kings 8:47).

I remember what I have received and heard. I hold fast, repent, and remain watchful (Rev. 3:3).

Let repentance and remission of sins be preached in Your name to all nations (Luke 24:47).

I repent before God and remain faithful toward my Lord Jesus Christ (Acts 20:21).

Godly sorrow produces repentance leading to salvation. I will not regret it (2 Cor. 7:10).

The Lord gives repentance to Israel and forgiveness of sins (Acts 5:31).

I will arise and go to my Father, and I will say to Him, "Father, I have sinned against heaven and before You" (Luke 15:18).

Prayers for Restoration and Revival

Lord, I thank You for restoration and revival. I thank You for showing me what is in my life that needs to come out if I am to walk in Your blessing and favor. I desire to have Your glory manifested in my life.

Lord, I pray that You would restore me and cause Your face to shine on me so that I will be delivered (Ps. 80:19).

Revive me again, O God, that I may rejoice in You (Ps. 85:6).

Lord, restore to me the joy of Your salvation and uphold me with Your willing spirit (Ps. 51:12).

Thank You, Lord, for restoring my soul and leading me in paths of righteousness for Your name's sake (Ps. 23:3).

Thank You, Lord, for restoring my fortunes (Jer. 49:6; Joel 3:1).

Restore me to Yourself, O Lord, that I may return! Renew my days as of old (Lam. 5:21).

Lord, thank You for sending the man and woman of God who truly come and restore all things (Matt. 17:11).

Let the house of the Lord be restored (2 Chron. 24:4).

Let the thief restore me sevenfold and give me back all the substance of my house (Prov. 6:31).

Let righteous judges be restored to my land, as they were at first. Let counselors come as they were at the beginning, that afterward we may be called the city of righteousness, a faithful town (Isa. 1:26).

Heal me, O God. Lead me and restore comfort to me (Isa. 57:18).

Restore the strength of Your people, O Lord (Lam. 1:11).

Thank You, Lord, that You have called me to Your eternal glory through Christ Jesus. Restore, support, strengthen, and establish me (1 Pet. 5:10).

Lord, I pray that You would restore all that was mine from the day that I abandoned it until now (2 Kings 8:6).

Lord, I thank You for those You have appointed to do the work in the house of the Lord, to repair and restore it (2 Chron. 34:10).

Lord, I pray that You would restore to Your people, even this day, their fields, their vineyards, their olive groves, and their houses, along with a hundredth part of the money, the grain, the wine, and the oil that they have lost (Neh. 5:11).

Lord, have mercy, for we are a people who have been robbed and despoiled; we have all been snared in holes and hidden in prison houses. We have become prey, and no one delivers us except You. We pray, "Please restore us" (Isa. 42:22).

Lord, thank You for Your Word: "For I will restore health to you, and I will heal you of your wounds…because they called you an outcast, saying, 'This is Zion whom no man cares for'" (Jer. 30:17). I recover this truth for my life in the name of Jesus.

Lord, I claim this truth for my life, my church, and my city: "I will restore the fortunes of My people Israel; they will rebuild the ruined cities and inhabit them; they will plant vineyards and drink their wine; they will make gardens and eat their fruit" (Amos 9:14).

Lord, I pray that You would restore to Your people a pure speech, that all of them may call on Your name to serve Him with one accord (Zeph. 3:9).

Chapter 10

New Things Spring Forth

> See, the former things have come to pass, and new things I declare; before they spring forth I tell you of them.
>
> —Isaiah 42:9

> Do not remember the former things nor consider the things of old. See, I will do a new thing, now it shall spring forth; shall you not be aware of it? I will even make a way in the wilderness, and rivers in the desert.
>
> —Isaiah 43:18–19

We have seen how prayer can sometimes begin with our needs and our concerns. But as we petition the throne of God and open ourselves to hear from Him, our prayers get bigger. We experience breakthrough and blessing in our lives. We are increased into larger realms of fruitfulness and prosperity. We begin to prophesy the goodness of the Lord and His power to deliver us from all our enemies. As with Hannah, our gratitude turns into a prophetic testimony, and we begin to prophesy God's goodness into the lives of others. We begin to see hope for our communities, our nation, and the world. We will also begin to see visions of revival sweeping the church.

Although we may go through dark seasons of desperation

personally, as we put our eyes on God, we begin to see that the desperate times extend beyond us and into the whole world. As we continue in prayer, God will show us His compassion for the world, and our prayers will begin to align with His plan to not only have His glory manifested in our lives but to have His glory fill the entire earth.

One of the key things in this process that we should not be too quick to bypass is what is actually happening to us—our character, our faith, our prayer life—in seasons of desperation. We've called it the desert and the wilderness based on our discussion about the children of Israel and their crossover from Egyptian slavery into the Promised Land. We've also seen it demonstrated as purging and cleansing in the story of Josiah's reign over Israel. Because this is such a critical time in the life of a believer, I want to share a few more points about this season before I get into the new things God will do. We will not be able to experience the bursting forth of those new things until we get what we are supposed to get from God in these desperate seasons.

The Good Thing About the Desert

In chapter 4 we discussed Israel's crossing over the Jordan from the wilderness to the Promised Land. We discovered that before they could cross over, many of those who left Egypt some forty years earlier died before they got to the Jordan. Israel is always a type for something in the spirit. I am sure that the loss of family members and loved ones while in the wilderness was painful. But I want you to see the spiritual significance of the dying. I mentioned that

God had passed judgment on them, and all those who were unbelieving had to die and a new, faithful generation had to be raised up before God would allow them to cross over into the promise He had set up for them.

In essence, God spoke to them and said, "No, you will not cross over in your current state—murmuring, complaining, and full of doubt. Before you come out of your desert place, your dry place, and before you go in to claim your possession, there are some things among you that must die. I have something more for you. And though My blessing is on you, you must stay in this place until those things die."

Some of you have been in a dry place. You've been walking around in circles in the wilderness, in a desert place. You know there is a promised land flowing with milk and honey; it has been prophesied over you for as long as you can remember. But you are where you are because God has to let some stuff die in you before you can cross over. For Israel, a whole generation had to die. For you in this season, God has things He needs to kill in you. Believe it or not, that's the good thing about the desert.

Some of us have so many things living in us that cannot be there if we want to go in and possess the land. It is God's grace that is saying, "You're not ready to go in, but I want to prepare you for it so that it will be a lasting and complete blessing to you and your generations to come. So I have to kill pride, vanity, selfishness, lust, doubt, fear, rebellion, stubbornness, and disobedience." These are the kinds of things that drop dead in the desert if you allow God to have His way.

Some of us fight this season. We try to hold on to the things that need to die, and they begin to kill us and our fire and hope in God. We let bitterness, anger, and rejection cause us to rise up against God in complaint. We become rebellious and disobedient. If you read Israel's account of their time in the wilderness, these are the attitudes you will find expressed among the generation that died.

We have their story so we can learn from it and not repeat what they did. Let the desert place do its divine work in your life. Do not despise the chastening of the Lord. As sons and daughters of God, we can look for His love and grace and favor even in desert seasons. Proverbs 3:11–12 says, "My son, do not despise the chastening of the LORD, nor be weary of His correction; for whom the LORD loves He corrects, even as a father the son in whom he delights."

We can get the mentality that God is not set against us but is preparing us for the place He has for us. We cannot go into the promised land with unbelief, disobedience, fear, ungratefulness, prayerlessness, powerlessness, and an inability to persist and press. The good thing about the desert is that we get to leave all of that behind and go into our promised land full of faith, submission, courage, and thanksgiving. Coming out of the desert, we are fixed, firmly planted, unshakeable, stable, established, and wise.

As we get this perspective during this season, it should be easy for us to accept the wisdom and timing of God in preparing us for a season of blessing and increase. We should be ready to let go of what needs to be discarded. Let die what needs to die. Let it go. Release it, whatever it is.

Circle until it's dead.

As you go through your desert season, there are times when it looks like you are going around in circles. You may feel like you have been at a similar place before. God doesn't want you to come back to the same place over and over again, repeating, rotating the same cycle, never getting ahead, never advancing, never going into the promised land. But if there are things you are holding on to and won't let go of, you have some circling to do. If you feel like you've been in the same place for too long and you can say, "I've been here before; this same thing keeps happening to me," it's time to get real and find out what needs to die.

Desert seasons are not meant to last forever. The Israelites were not supposed to be in the wilderness for forty years. According to some accounts, the trip from Egypt to Canaan was only a few days' journey. But God kept them there until all doubt and disobedience were dead. Once they were clear of that, God told Israel that their cycle in the wilderness was coming to an end. And this is when Moses released a new word into that next generation: "May the LORD, the God of your fathers, make you one thousand times more numerous and bless you, just as He has promised you" (Deut. 1:11). This is the thousands blessing Moses released over the people just before he died. They were coming out of the desert and getting ready to enter the Promised Land, and he prophesied a whole new level of blessing and increase over them.

God is going to do the same for you as you come out of this season of challenge and hardship. You are coming out. Let what has to die, die now. If it's unbelief, let it die so you can stop circling the wilderness year after year. If you need to begin to speak to your situation, do it. Bind the devil. Rebuke the recurring-cycle demon. Do not allow him to cause you to think that dry seasons are the norm in the life of a believer. They are not. Righteousness is. Joy is. Peace is. (See Romans 14:17.)

It does not have to take forty years of your life for things to die. Let it die, and let it die quickly. And then let God release a new word to you.

A New Song and a New Word

In Isaiah 42:9 God tells us, "See, the former things have come to pass, and new things I declare; before they spring forth I tell you of them." And in Isaiah 43:19 He says, "See, I will do a new thing, now it shall spring forth; shall you not be aware of it? I will even make a way in the wilderness, and rivers in the desert." I like that term *spring forth*. It reads as if the new things that God wants to do are going to come up from out of the ground. It's as if we will begin to see plants springing forth, buds springing forth from the trees. We will begin to see something that looked like it was dead spring forth into new life. We will see trees that looked like they were dead, with all the leaves fallen off—no green anywhere—but all of a sudden new buds will spring forth. I think this is exactly what God is saying to us, but from a spiritual perspective. These verses relay to us a prophetic word from God about His doing something new and fresh in our lives.

Then God says, "Before it happens, I will declare it unto you." This is why the prophetic is so important. This is also why I like being around prophets and prophetic people. When God is about to do something new in your life, He will release a new word to you. You will begin to hear God again for yourself and for others. Didn't we see this with Hannah? After breaking through and bearing a son, she received a new word from God and released it in 1 Samuel 2.

God will tell you what He's going to do before He does it because He wants you to know that it was He who did it and not you. As a matter of fact, I also believe the prophetic word not only informs you about what's about to happen, but it also activates the new thing that is to spring forth. That's why when you are truly prophetic and are around prophetic people, there's always something new coming forth in your life. It's the nature of the prophetic.

When you're prophetic, you should never, ever get stuck in a rut with nothing happening. There should always be something new springing forth in your life. It could be a new relationship, a new city, a new door, a new ministry, new people, new connections, a new level, a new revelation, a new anointing, new finances, new breakthroughs, new favor, or new blessings. There are so many new things God can do in your life.

With a prophetic connection with God and other believers, you live with the expectation of new things always coming into your life. You will know that from the foundation of the world God has planned some things for your life. They may not happen all at once, but as you live your life, God unfolds them one by one—He causes them to spring forth. And sometimes He saves the best for last, like when He turned water into wine. (See John 2:1–10.) The wedding guests asked the host, "Why did you save your best wine till last?" In most cases, it is recommended to put out the best wine first, but Jesus saved the best wine for last.

God always brings us into new things because His plan

for our lives is never fulfilled in just a short period of time. So don't be discouraged if you are in a time of testing and trial. It will not last forever. Seasons come to an end. Winter gives way to spring. If you do what God tells us to do, if you complete this current season with faith and obedience, you will come out of this dry place. Realize that the new thing is for people who do something with the old thing and who were faithful and obedient in the previous season. If this is you, continue to expect God to birth new things in your life. They will spring forth.

A New You

Not only will a new thing spring forth in your life, but a new you will be formed to handle it. We've already talked about this concerning the wilderness. That time of testing and trial is part of the process of forming the new you. Let's look again at Isaiah 43:18–21 (emphasis added):

> Do not remember the former things nor consider the things of old. See, I will do a new thing, now it shall spring forth; shall you not be aware of it? I will even make a way in the wilderness, and rivers in the desert. The beast of the field shall honor Me, the jackals and the owls, because I give waters in the wilderness, and rivers in the desert, to give drink to My people, My chosen ones. *This people I have formed for Myself*; they shall declare My praise.

These verses provide a very interesting revelation. They tell us that when God does a new thing, He also forms a new people. And when He forms this new people, they will declare His praise. You will always know when God is doing something new in your life because there will always be a new praise. As a matter of fact, you will be a new person. This doesn't mean you have to change physically and meet all new people. But when God does a new thing, you become new. Can you see how this is true? Think about where you are now and what God is asking of you. Are there things He wants you to let go of? Are there areas in which He is challenging you to grow? Are there new opportunities or new people He wants you to have the courage to embrace? The things that call us to stretch beyond what is comfortable, that may feel somewhat painful, are the things that transform us into new people who are ready for God's new thing.

In thinking about this transformation, I am reminded of my church, Crusaders Ministries, and the history of how we began in a small storefront. We were part of the Church of God in Christ denomination. We were Pentecostal and Holiness. We did things a certain way. We were a bunch of young people who loved God. I was twenty-one when I came into the church, and my wife, Wanda, was only sixteen when she joined. As we moved into the 1980s, God began to form us into a completely new people. Every time we thought we'd made it, God would bring something new. We came into the Word of Faith movement. We became a church that focused on deliverance. Then we became a prophetic people, and next an apostolic people. We became a revival and a glory people and then a kingdom people. The new things of God kept springing forth. It's almost like every time God did something new in our church, we became a new church. We are not the same as we used to be. We have become a new people.

Some people could not handle the new things God brought us into season after season, and they chose to leave. Some people don't want to change. But new people were always coming in while some of the older people left. God was forming a new congregation because He wanted His glory to rest among us.

God is always doing a new thing, which calls us to be made into a new people. When God revealed to us His plan for delivering His people from the torment of the enemy—which is what deliverance is—it was new. It was fresh. We were excited. God had formed us into a new church and a new people who could handle this new mantle. With every change from that point on, God continually formed and re-formed us into new people—taking us from faith to faith and glory to glory—who could handle the movement of His Spirit and His heart for transforming the community around us.

While I know everyone can't make these changes with us, I find that the new things in God are exciting. I like new things, even in the natural—new clothes, new shoes, new cars, new homes. When you go to the store and buy something new, it makes you feel good. A new shirt, a new tie, a new look, a new sound—I like new things, because new things stir us and keep us excited. They make life worth living.

The people who knew you when...

We often use 2 Corinthians 5:17—"If any man is in Christ, he is a new creature. Old things have passed away.

Look, all things have become new"—when we are talking about salvation, but it applies to all the levels of newness that God brings us to throughout our lives with Him. Old things pass away. You become a new creature. You become different. *All* things become new. Every part of your life changes. The way you look at things becomes new. The way you live becomes new.

Sometimes people like to stick you in a box and make you stay there because they know the way you were five or ten years ago. They want to hold you down and limit you. They say, "Oh, I know you. I remember when you were this and when you were that." They don't want to let you go because they can't handle change.

But God says, "No, I'm not going to let you get stuck. I am not going to let you be limited by what people think. I will do something new. I will break you out of that limitation and box. I'm not going to let people stick you in a box and leave you there."

Sometimes the worst people to deal with are those who have known you the longest. When you go outside the house or the place where everyone is most familiar with you, you are celebrated. When you come back home, it's like you are nobody. One time I went to India, and they celebrated my coming with fireworks. That never happened to me before. They said, "Before you go in the church, stop outside." As I was going into the building to minister, they started shooting fireworks. That's usually for the Fourth of July. I felt so special. I was waiting for the national anthem.

Then I came back to Chicago, and people were not excited: "Oh, that's John Eckhardt. We knew him when he was on Channel 38 hosting that TV show *Perfecting the*

Saints. Yeah, he pastors that deliverance church down there on 38th and Michigan. Yeah, we know him." These were the people who hadn't seen me or spoken with me in years, but they thought they knew me. Have you ever experienced this? It reminds me of the verse that says, "No prophet is accepted in his own country" (Luke 4:24).

There's One who really does know you. He knows your end from your beginning. He knows the seasons you go through. He knows the changes you go through. He remembers when you first got saved and when you got baptized in the Holy Spirit. He remembers when you got the call to the ministry. He knows you so well that He also knows when it is time to do a new thing in your life. He knows how to change you for that new thing too. Can you trust Him with these changes? Can you trust Him when people who want you to stay the same start to speak against what God is doing in your life?

Can you imagine what Joseph's brothers thought when they sold him? (See Genesis 37 and 42 for this portion of Joseph's story.) He was their younger brother, and they had gotten mad when he told them about his dream. But then they ended up standing before him years later, and he was the prime minister of Egypt. He was not the same Joseph they stuck in a pit. He was not the boy they knew when they sold him to the Egyptians.

See, Joseph had something new coming into his life. God told him about it first, then orchestrated his life in a way that would prepare him to handle what he had been shown in the dream. God took him from Potiphar's house to the prison house to the palace.

When Joseph told his brothers about the new thing God

was going to do and that they would be bowing down, they got mad. But years later, there they were, living in a fulfilled prophecy and bowing down to their brother, the prime minister. God had changed him, and they were afraid and thought they were in trouble for how they had treated him. Everything had changed in Joseph's life, even his old relationships.

Changes like this are sometimes very hard for people. But resistance to change, including resistance to increase and going to the next level, makes us resistant to the new things God wants to do. I want to encourage you to remain open. The new things are worth the risk of losing the old. Let God make everything new.

Same Place, Same Problems

Being in a place in your life when nothing new happens feels terrible. It's as if you are stuck in the same place with the same problems. At least if you are going to have problems, let them be new. It sounds funny, and you may laugh and say, "I don't want any new problems." But what about this new problem: You know how there are certain problems that come with being poor? There is a whole other set of problems that come when you get a lot of money. Would you rather have rich problems or poor problems? With poor problems, you can't pay your bills, you may be at risk of losing your home, and no one answers your calls because they don't want to lend you money. With rich problems, everybody is calling you.

Some of us have had the same problems for the last fifteen

years. Wouldn't it be great to be at a different place in life where new things are happening, even with the new levels of problems and responsibilities that come with them? Yes, get some rich problems. Get some Oprah Winfrey–level problems. Yes, she has problems too.

When you get wealth, you have to handle your money. That can be a problem. Everybody wants your money. You may even need security because you have so much. You know, Oprah Winfrey can't even go into a store. She has to shut stores down just to go shopping. Michael Jackson used to put on disguises to go shopping. Can you imagine having to disguise yourself just to go shopping because everybody wants your autograph or photo? If you're like me and some people I know, you have the opposite problem. When we go to the store, we can't find help. We have to ask: "Is somebody here? How much does this cost? Does anybody work here?" They don't pay us any attention.

I'm being funny about this, but the point here is that with new things come new levels of concern and responsibility. Some people actually avoid new things for this very reason. They would rather stay where they are in the life they are living, with no changes. They want to keep the same problems they have. They don't want anything to change. This is the reason we have to be transformed—so we are open to the new things God has for us.

Let God Do Something New

When God is planning to do something new in our lives, He has a plan to make us new as well. We cannot remain the same if we allow God to do a new thing. We may have the same name and may physically look the same, but we are not the same. Something happens. God changes us. One of the worst things is when I see people after a long time and nothing has changed in their lives. They're still saying the same things, still believing for the same things. There is no growth and no new perspective. They are closed to God doing something new in their lives.

I always want God to do something new in my life. I'm not the same pastor and preacher I was twenty-five years ago. God has done something in my life. He has brought new things into my life, and He has changed me because of them.

One of the best compliments you can receive is when someone says, "Something new has happened to you. You seem different. God has done something fresh. I sense it in you." It's not that you are trying to impress anyone, but they can sense God has done something new. This is a good thing. It doesn't mean that what you were was bad. It simply means that as you move and grow in God, the changes in you are evident. You bear witness to the fact that God always has something new and fresh He wants to do in our lives.

Things in our world are always changing. Companies, governments, nations, and even generations change. But sometimes we as believers don't really change, and as a result we become obsolete, outdated, and outmoded. We lose our freshness and then wonder why the church isn't growing. I encourage you to yield to God as He works to transform you into a new person who can move in new things. I encourage you to be open to being part of a movement instead of becoming a monument. If we resist the new things of God, we can easily become obsolete.

People need change; they need something new—and they look for it. They're not going to walk into a building where the same old songs and sounds from thirty years ago are still sung and heard. They want something fresh and new because they have changed. But often our churches get stuck; the presentation remains the same, and we miss the new thing and being open to receive the new people who need God's new things in their lives as well.

God of the New Thing

God likes new things. He is the God of new things. We tend to think that because God is ancient (Daniel 7:9 says He is the Ancient of Days) and has been around forever, somehow that means He is stuck in the past. But God is a God who creates new things. He causes the sun to rise, and there's always a new day. There's always a new sunset. There's always a new spring. There's always a new summer. There's always a new fall. There's always a new season. There's always a new generation. There are always new children, new fruit, new flowers, and new plants. There's always something new, because God created even the earth to represent the part of His character that always desires newness. Just as it is in the natural, so is it in the spirit.

As you've been reading this book, and even as you may be living through a difficult season, I pray that your faith is growing stronger so you can hear and receive this word: God is about to cause something to spring forth in your life that you've never had before. Your winter season is over, and a new spring season is coming. It's about to be released. I prophesy it to you today. Get ready for some new things to be released in your life. Get ready to spring ahead both in the natural and in the spirit.

You Need New Things in Your Life

I'm learning this: the older we get, the more we need new things in our lives. They keep us going. Age is physical, but it also has a lot to do with your mentality. You can begin to think and act old. You can think that you've done everything and there is nothing new for you to do or experience; you've done it all and seen it all. You've been to all kinds of church services. You've heard the best preachers ministering under powerful anointings. You've seen powerful demonstrations of the laying on of hands where people have fallen under the power of God. You've seen people healed and have heard amazing prophecy. You've read all the books, listened to all the recordings, heard all the teachings, and been to all of the workshops. There is nothing else. You've done it all. These are the kinds of people I see sleeping in church.

This is not OK. Where is the openness? Where is the teachability? Where is the humility? None of us know it all. None of us have done it all. There is always more. Don't get caught in this place. Being open to God and the new things He wants to do. It will keep us young and vibrant in the spirit, and humble and zealous in His presence. Don't let the enemy trick you into thinking there is nothing else for you and that you have experienced all there is to experience. You will be like so many others who have set themselves up on thrones of leviathan—a high place where you see yourself as having experienced all there is to experience in God.

As we mature in God we can still enjoy the new thing He is doing. You can be older in the natural but young in the spirit if you stay open to new things. I have seen seventy- and eighty-year-olds still praising God, dancing up and down the aisle, enjoying the new things of God. It blesses me to see older members still prophesying and getting the word of the Lord. They haven't retired and given up. They're keeping themselves in an atmosphere where they are challenged to believe that God is going to do something new and fresh in their lives and the lives of those around them. They're always ready to receive the new thing that God is doing. I like that.

You Need a New Environment

I encourage you to look at your environment. Are you in a place that challenges you to believe God for new things? I mentioned earlier that a strong prophetic atmosphere where people are always seeking to hear from God is one where the expectation is always high for new things. In an environment where the word of the Lord flows freely and unhindered, you will not be able to stay down for long. Just when you are at your lowest point, you are discouraged, nothing is moving, you think it's over, and everything seems dead, that is when someone steps up and tells you, "Thus saith the Lord: it's not over yet. God says He's going to do this and that in your life."

Sometimes that word hits you in your belly and you fall out weeping because you recognize that God has not forgotten about you. The devil may have told you that God is finished with you, that nothing will happen and nothing will change. He may have been whispering in your ear, and you've been agreeing with him until the prophet steps up and gives you a word from the Lord. A word at the right time will shake something loose in your life and cause you to believe again. It will strengthen you. It will bring a fresh wind. It will refresh you in the desert place.

Just as God promised, He is going to put water in your desert place. He is going to cause streams and rivers to flow where there was no water and no life. Where there was death and barrenness, He is going to cause new life to spring forth. I like that. This is the kind of uplifting you will find in the company of prophets and prophetic believers.

Get to a church that believes in prophetic ministry and a releasing of the word of the Lord. Let someone minister to you and speak the word of the Lord over your life. Let the prophetic minister to you and lift you up in this season. Prophecy is for the edification and building up of one another.

The New Thing Is About God's Glory Revealed in You

I don't care what kind of pit or prison you're in, in this season; God will change your situation and do a new thing in your life. Like He did with Joseph, God will put you in a place where your brethren won't even recognize you. Some people may be upset when they see what God is going to do with your life. But it's not you; it's God. He has had a plan for your life from the foundation of the world. And when you get to that place and see the people who mocked you, laughed at you, sold you out, and spoke against God's plan, you will be able to forgive them, bless them, and minister to them, just as Joseph did.

If you haven't gotten it already, let me break it down: This new thing that God wants to do is not only about you; it's about Him. It's not about you being big. It's about His purposes. God is not doing it just for you. He's doing it for Himself.

God has plans He needs to accomplish in the earth, and He needs new people—delivered and restored people—who will partner with Him to bring them down from heaven to earth. God has some things He needs done in America and around the world, and He can't do it with the old wineskin. He needs a new wineskin. He has to pour some new things in you, and right now you're not able to handle the new thing He wants to do. If God poured new wine in you now, you'd burst. God has assignments and commissions to hand off to you that you cannot complete in the condition you are in and with the mentality you have.

God is saying, "I can't use you the way you are. The way you think, believe, and act, the level you're on—I can't use you right now. What I have for you is so much bigger and so much greater, and you can't move in it just yet. There are some places I want you to go that you are not ready for. There are some doors I want to open up for you, but you are not yet ready to walk through them. There are some people I want you to talk to, but you are not yet on the level to talk to them." God has some assignments that are high, and you can't move into them right now without first being transformed.

Once you are changed, though, the new thing will not be delayed. It will spring forth. You will move into that new assignment. You will be able to do what you could not do before. You will walk into places where you could not walk before. Again, this is the purpose of the desert place or the wilderness. It is perfecting in you the humility, wisdom, compassion, forgiveness, patience, perseverance, and all the fruit of the Spirit you need to possess and maintain the new thing and bring glory to God.

When you understand this, then He will release to you new revelation, power, anointing, skill, and favor. Because you have aligned with God, new things are going to spring forth in your life. The dry ground will be watered. Fruitfulness, favor, grace, increase, blessing, and prosperity will return, and you will release a new level of praise. You will prophesy again, and the windows of heaven will be opened to you.

Prayers to Activate New Things

Lord, I declare that the former things have come to pass. Now I receive the new things that will spring forth (Isa. 42:9).

I will not call to my mind the former things or ponder the things of the past. I look to the new things that the Lord will do. They will spring forth even now (Isa. 43:18–19).

I receive new things from this time and not what was created long ago. I receive even the hidden things I have not known (Isa. 48:6–8).

I am a new creature in Christ. Old things have passed away. All things have become new (2 Cor. 5:17).

I will sing a new song unto the Lord, for He has done marvelous things (Ps. 98:1).

Behold, You make all things new (Rev. 21:5).

Lord, bring new things to me out of Your treasures (Matt. 13:52).

Lord, put new wine in new bottles for me, that both may be preserved (Luke 5:38).

I look for new heavens and a new earth that You have promised (2 Pet. 3:13).

Lord, put within me a new heart and a new spirit. Take away my stony heart and give me a heart of flesh (Ezek. 36:26).

Let my barns be filled with plenty and my presses burst with new wine (Prov. 3:10).

I put on the new man, which is created after God in righteousness and true holiness (Eph. 4:24).

I purge out the old leaven, that I may be a new lump (1 Cor. 5:7).

By a new and living way, I draw near to God with a true heart in full assurance of faith (Heb. 10:20–22).

Lord, write for me a new commandment, because the darkness is past, and true light shines (1 John 2:8).

Declarations and Decrees for New Things

Lord, I believe You are the God of the new thing, and I declare today new beginnings. New things will begin to spring forth in my life.

As I declare it, as I decree it, I believe for new things to happen for me.

This is a new season. This is a new day. This is a new time. I decree it now.

I speak new strength, new power, new authority, and new joy into my life.

New vision, new dreams, new ideas, new thoughts, a new mind, and a new way of thinking do I decree in my life.

New favor is coming upon me.

New grace, new mercy, new compassion, new love, new faith, and new hope are coming into my life.

I decree and declare new relationships, new people, new friends, and new opportunities are coming into my life, and new doors are opening for me.

In the name of Jesus, new finances, new business, new prosperity, and new money are coming my way.

I decree new songs, new praise, new worship, new anointing, new breakthroughs, new levels, new revelation, new understanding, and new wisdom. Let them all be released in my life, in the name of Jesus.

And for Your church, O God: new breath, new wind, new spirit, new moves of God, new sounds, new ministries, new people, new souls, new teachings, new music, new glory, new miracles, new signs, new wonders, new healings, new deliverances, new salvations, new members, new teams being raised up, and more. Let them be released.

And for Your people: new cars, new homes, new clothes, new jobs, new things, new businesses, new land, new property, new accounts, new beauty, new glory, new honor, new positions, new mantles, new assignments, new commissions, new prayer language, new tongues, new boldness, new courage, new ability, and new giftings, in the name of Jesus. Let them be released.

And for Your kingdom: new nations, new cities, new regions, new territories, and new churches. Let them be released.

Father, I believe that as I declare and as I decree, these new things will begin to manifest starting today and in the days and months and years to come.

I believe You will do a new thing in my life. The old is passing away. The new thing is arising. New blessings are being released in my life, in the name of Jesus.

With my words and with my mouth, I decree new things, in the name of Jesus, and I believe, expect, and look for these new things to be established.

A New Season

Prophetic Poem by John Eckhardt

Those who prepared themselves for the new
shall enter the new door and go through.

Into a new place you will stand
and receive the best from My hand.

I will let you see a side of Me you have never seen before.
My glory you shall see and receive blessings even more.

This is the season you will see.
The things you have believed for will manifest for thee.

The time you have worshipped has not been a waste of time.
These times have proven that you are truly Mine.

Because you belong to Me, I will show
My blessings and favor you will truly know.

So rejoice and enter into a new season, My chosen ones,
And enjoy the blessings that are to come.

I speak to those who have ears to hear,
And by My Spirit I draw you near.

So continue to worship in the season that is new
And watch the wonders I will do.

Notes

Chapter 1
Your Name Is Favor

1. "How Many Wives Did King David Have?," GotQuestions .com, accessed May 2, 2018, https://www.gotquestions.org /wives-King-David.html.
2. Blue Letter Bible, s.v. "Commentary on 1 Kings 11," accessed May 2, 2018, https://www.blueletterbible.org /Comm/jfb/1Ki/1Ki_011.cfm?a=302003.
3. Blue Letter Bible, s.v. "*Channah*," accessed May 2, 2018, https://www.blueletterbible.org/lang/lexicon/lexicon.cfm ?t=kjv&strongs=h2584; s.v. "*chanan*," accessed May 2, 2018, https://www.blueletterbible.org/lang/lexicon/lexicon .cfm?Strongs=H2603.
4. Blue Letter Bible, s.v. "*chen*," accessed May 2, 2018, https://www.blueletterbible.org/lang/lexicon/lexicon.cfm ?strongs=H2580; s.v. "*charis*," accessed May 2, 2018, https://www.blueletterbible.org/lang/lexicon/lexicon.cfm ?strongs=G5485.
5. Blue Letter Bible, s.v. "*charisma*," accessed May 2, 2018, https://www.blueletterbible.org/lang/lexicon/lexicon.cfm ?Strongs=G5486&t=KJV.
6. Oxford Living Dictionaries, s.v. "favour," accessed August 23, 2017, https://en.oxforddictionaries.com/definition /favour.
7. David Reagan, "Favor of God," LearntheBible.org, accessed August 23, 2017, http://www.learnthebible.org /favor-of-god.html.
8. *Merriam-Webster*, s.v. "favor," accessed May 2, 2018, https://www.merriam-webster.com/dictionary/favor.

9. John Eckhardt, *Ridiculous Favor* (Chicago, IL: John Eckhardt Ministries, 2017), xi–xii.

10. John Eckhardt, *God's Covenant With You for Deliverance and Freedom* (Lake Mary, FL: Charisma House, 2014).

11. Blue Letter Bible, s.v. "*heykal*," accessed May 2, 2018, https://www.blueletterbible.org/lang/lexicon/lexicon.cfm?Strongs=H1964&t=KJV.

12. Blue Letter Bible, s.v. "*barak*," accessed May 2, 2018, https://www.blueletterbible.org/lang/lexicon/lexicon.cfm?Strongs=H1288&t=KJV.

13. Emily Barnhardt, "Weeping in Worship," Joyful31.com, May 5, 2016, http://joyful31.com/2016/05/05/weeping-in-worship/.

Chapter 2
When Desperation Becomes Your Friend

1. Blue Letter Bible, s.v. "*'anag*," accessed May 2, 2018, https://www.blueletterbible.org/lang/lexicon/lexicon.cfm?Strongs=H6026&t=KJV.

Chapter 3
The Power of Persevering Prayer

1. *Merriam-Webster*, s.v. "devote," accessed May 2, 2018, https://www.merriam-webster.com/dictionary/devote.

2. See John Eckhardt, *Unshakeable* (Lake Mary, FL: Charisma House, 2015) and John Eckhardt, *Destroying the Spirit of Rejection* (Lake Mary, FL: Charisma House, 2016).

3. Thomas Hauser, "The Unforgiven," *The Guardian*, September 3, 2005, https://www.theguardian.com/sport/2005/sep/04/features.sport16.

4. Associated Press, "Twelve-Round Limit for WBC," *New York Times*, December 10, 1982, https://www.nytimes.com/1982/12/10/sports/12-round-limit-for-wbc.html.

Chapter 4
Crossing Over

1. Blue Letter Bible, s.v. "*yashab*," accessed May 2, 2018, https://www.blueletterbible.org/lang/lexicon/lexicon.cfm?t=kjv&strongs=h3427.
2. *Merriam-Webster*, s.v. "inhabit," accessed May 2, 2018, https://www.merriam-webster.com/dictionary/inhabit.

Chapter 5
A Thousand Times More

1. Blue Letter Bible, s.v. "Deuteronomy," accessed May 2, 2018, https://www.blueletterbible.org/search/Dictionary/viewTopic.cfm?topic=ET0001024,HT0000649,IT0002669,BT0001162.

Chapter 7
When the Glory Comes

1. Blue Letter Bible, s.v. "'*erets*," accessed May 2, 2018, https://www.blueletterbible.org/lang/lexicon/lexicon.cfm?Strongs=H776&t=KJV.
2. John Eckhardt, *Prayers That Rout Demons* (Lake Mary, FL: Charisma House, 2008), 43–44.
3. John Eckhardt, *Prayers That Move Mountains* (Lake Mary, FL: Charisma House, 2012), 56–60.

Chapter 8
The Prayers of the Saints

1. "The Court of the Women in the Temple," Bible-History.com, accessed April 30, 2018, http://www.bible-history.com/court-of-women/.
2. "The Court of the Women in the Temple," Bible-History.com.

Chapter 9
Then Comes Revival

1. Eckhardt, *Prayers That Move Mountains*, 54–56.